# DOCTOR WHO

## THE EARLY YEARS

D1490180

# THE EARLY YEARS

## Jeremy Bentham

W.H. ALLEN · LONDON
1986

Typeset by Phoenix Photosetting, Chatham, Kent
Printed and bound in Great Britain by
Mackays of Chatham Ltd, Kent
for the Publishers, W.H. Allen & Co. Plc
44 Hill Street, London W1X 8LB

Reprinted, May 1986, December 1987

*British Library Cataloguing in Publication Data*

Bentham, Jeremy
Doctor Who, the early years.
1. Doctor Who (Television program)
I. Title
791.45'72      PN1992.77.D6/

ISBN 0 491 03612 4

## Acknowledgements

Researching a book of this complexity would not have been
possible without the help, advice and support of a great many
people connected in and around the *Doctor Who* series. On the
visual side I would like to thank, first and foremost, Ray Cusick,
whose work I admired as a child and which is now, at long last,
getting the recognition it so richly deserves. Special thanks also to
Phil Bevan and Susan Moore for other stills used in this book.

On the text side I should like to record my gratitude to the
writers and researchers of the CMS *Space and Time* Project
(particularly Gary, Tim, Dave and Steve) whose efforts over the
last six years have provided much of the invaluable background
material used in this book. Additional thanks to Sydney Newman,
Verity Lambert, Carole Ann Ford, June Barry, Stephanie
Whitaker, Peter Haining, Ian Levine, Deanne Holding and, from
the BBC, Glyn Martin, Irene Basterfield and the girls of the
Drama Script Unit.

Lastly, very special thanks are due to Christopher Barry whose
own photographic and reference material have enhanced this book
far beyond my original estimations, and to Editor Nigel Robinson
for getting the whole endeavour off the ground in the first place.

*J. Jeremy Bentham*
August 1985

**Dedication**

'I think that if I live to be ninety, a little of the magic of *Doctor Who* will still cling to me'

William Hartnell,
the Original Doctor
1908–1975

This book is dedicated to Sydney Newman and to the memory of David Whitaker and William Hartnell – the Man, Myth and Magic of *Doctor Who*.

And also to Paully and Phil: much needed islands of sanity and insanity.

# CONTENTS

# RAYMOND P. CUSICK

NOW A SENIOR Designer for the BBC, Raymond Cusick started his post-graduate career as an art teacher. Seeking more of a challenge in life he became a Designer in Repertory Theatre for three years before applying to join the BBC's Design Department in 1960. He was accepted as a Design Assistant and became a Designer proper in 1962.

Up until *Doctor Who* entered his life in the Autumn of 1963 he worked on many productions, none of them major, and frequently in the area of Light Entertainment, on shows such as *Sykes* and *Hugh And I*.

*Doctor Who* came his way almost by accident when he was called upon to replace fellow Designer Ridley Scott, later to direct *Alien*, who had to drop out at the last minute. For the next two years he worked solidly on the programme, sharing the enormous task of designing sets, visual effects and special props in the main with only one other Designer, Barry Newbery.

Due to his position as a BBC staff member Raymond Cusick received none of the millions of pounds in royalties generated in the wake of the Daleks' international success, his sole consolation being a one-off Special Merit payment, even then made only after a hard-fought campaign by his Head of Department.

Designer Ray Cusick and 'friends'.

Raymond Cusick describes himself as a 'drama man' with an interest in history, especially social history and the history of aviation. Since leaving *Doctor Who*, vowing never to return, he has had many opportunities to indulge his interests, working on many highly acclaimed period dramas, such as *The Pallisers*, *The Duchess Of Duke Street*, *The Gathering Seed*, *When The Boat Comes In*, *To Serve Them All My Days* and recently the successful *Miss Marple* series.

Although expressing no preference for science fiction, he has been able to turn his hand to whatever is asked, and his sf output includes the classic 'Get Off My Cloud' episode of *Out Of The Unknown* which, totally by coincidence, featured one of his Daleks and the TARDIS prop.

Together with his wife, Cusick is also the proprietor of a small hotel in South London where he keeps many of the constructional drawings, paintings and props he designed for *Doctor Who* between 1963 and 1966. This book represents first publication of these drawings and paintings, including the blueprints of the sixties' Dalek machine itself. Along with his immense collection of photographs covering the behind-the-scenes making of the stories he worked on, they comprise a unique insight into the very early years of BBC's *Doctor Who* series.

10

# JEREMY BENTHAM

FASCINATED SINCE childhood by the *Doctor Who* television series, Jeremy Bentham was a co-founder of the British Appreciation Society in May 1976 when he used his large collection of *Doctor Who* documentation as the basis for its Reference Department.

He was principal writer for the *Doctor Who Weekly* publication on its launch in 1979, rising eventually to the post of Associate Editor when it turned monthly in 1980.

He has collaborated on several *Doctor Who* books for W.H. Allen over the years, most notably Peter Haining's *Doctor Who: A Celebration*. For the TV show's twentieth anniversary in 1983, he co-organised the British Film Institute's *Doctor Who* weekend at the National Film Theatre in London.

With a declared interest in computers, Jeremy lives in Hendon, North London.

Jeremy Bentham.

# INTRODUCTION

TELEVISION IS the most powerful tool of communication the world
has ever known. No other medium, not even a combination of
press, radio, cinema and theatre together, enables the few to
impart to the many with quite the force, the immediacy, and the
popularity of Television.

Once described as 'the flickering eye', the images dancing from
the television cathode ray tube are every bit as fascinating as the
jewelled pendant swung back and forth by the hand of an
experienced hypnotist. Television compels its viewers to pay
attention whether they like it or not. Most often situated at the
focal point of any room's layout, the constant bombardment of
ever-changing light and sound virtually prohibits any other kind of
thought-demanding activity while the educating, informing or
entertaining process is in motion. With seats usually positioned to
face the screen, any casual entrants to a room are given every
encouragement to latch their eyes, ears and concentration onto the
programmes being screened. And once attention is grabbed the
real magic of the spell begins.

Television's greatest power is its power of illusion; to convince the viewer that what they are seeing is real, no matter how fantastic the concept. When a dramatic fight sequence is acted out on screen no thought is given, by the viewer, to the scene's background. The many days the actor spent learning his script are invisible. So too are the endless hours spent arduously rehearsing in church halls. The practice run-throughs, the strict choreography of the action, the careful planning of the Director to ensure safety, all this is lost to the audience at home. All they feel is either revulsion at a particularly violent sequence, or an excited catharsis as the morally wrong are given their due come-uppance.

The key-note to all television drama is suspension of disbelief. That the success rate is almost one hundred per-cent every day is a tribute to the whole structure of television presentation – from the writing of words on a blank sheet of paper, to the transmission of broadcast signals through the air.

*Doctor Who* needs no introduction to this principle. Indeed, right from its very first episode it has relied upon that elusive quality to convince its audiences that even the most far-fetched adventures are as acceptably believable as any down-to-earth example of *cinéma verité*.

Of course, if the viewer sits back and thinks about it, any *Doctor Who* episode is absurd. Man has hardly set foot on the Moon, let alone gone voyaging in search of the mythical lost civilisation of the Cybermen. What is presented on screen is a plywood set, lit by studio arc lamps, populated by Equity member actors wearing costumes sewn together by the talents of the Wardrobe Department.

Yet all that is perpetually transparent. Somewhere between a studio stage and the story-weaving imagination of the writer is the middle ground of perception where reality meets fantasy and acceptance is subconsciously defined and agreed.

In *Doctor Who*'s case, this means applying a greater number of mental masks than those required, say, to watch an episode of *Jewel In The Crown*, which, in turn, requires more than for an episode of *Juliet Bravo*.

In the latter instance the characters and social settings are familiar from everyday life, and so suspension of disbelief is easy. With *Jewel In The Crown* the perception threshold needs amending to cater for a television screen acting as a window into Earth's past. And thus, for *Doctor Who*, thresholds need still further restructuring so that a viewer might mentally walk beside the Doctor on his explorations of an alien planet without thoughts intruding as to the implausibility of it all.

Generally, the older the viewer, the harder it is to apply these masks, especially where fantasy and science fiction are concerned. Correspondingly, audiences for sf and fantasy adventure tend towards the younger end of the market.

*Doctor Who*, though, is the exception, and has been right from its starting point. Somehow it succeeds in grabbing and holding a 'family audience', television parlance for a term implying viewers under seven to over seventy in age grouping. How it manages this

quite remarkable feat is a question that has kept many television researchers and historians intrigued for years, for, by and large, *Doctor Who* is nowhere near as slick and glossy as many of its more obvious, would-be sf competitors.

In 1966, *Doctor Who* faced the challenge of *Thunderbirds*, a very innovative puppet series with miniatures and model effects work that were the envy of the world. In 1975, it was up against *Space 1999*, then the highest-budgeted series on television. More recently, in 1980, came *Buck Rogers In The 25th Century*, challenging the Doctor's storylines with its arsenal of special effects, grandiose locations and leggy '*Barbie-doll*' female guest stars.

Surviving and outliving all these challengers, *Doctor Who* has emerged triumphant, becoming one of Britain's most highly exported programmes during the mid-1980s. The perception thresholds for watching the show, it appears, know no international boundaries.

The format of *Doctor Who* is what gives the show its enormous strength. It is very flexible, offering authors greater freedoms than would normally be allowed writing for other programmes. Over the years this prospectus has attracted some of the top names in the writing field, among them Dennis Spooner (of *The Professionals*), movie-screen writers Mervyn Haisman and Henry Lincoln, *Bergerac* creator Robert Banks Stewart and Galactic Hitch-Hiker Douglas Adams. Even the list of authors whose stories never made it to the screen are impressive, including such names as Christopher Priest and Tanith Lee.

Yet writing for *Doctor Who* is only part of the process, albeit a very important one. It defines as a very insular activity, involving, per story, really only two people – the author (a freelance writer) and the Script Editor (a resident BBC employee). Although working to a discipline, and with an eye on costs and practicality, theirs is still, primarily, the realm of imagination, where the only restrictions are those of creativity and inventiveness. Their tools are the typewriter and a box of blank paper, from which emerge the fifty-page average *Doctor Who* episode script. Only when that is ready does the real magic of Television take over.

The analogy of magic to Television is not misplaced. To the uninitiated, entering the control room, or 'gallery', of a television studio is every bit as daunting as stepping into the lair of some mystic practitioner. Arrays of coloured lights, switches and buttons assault the eye, each labelled with curious cabalistic symbols. The gallery crew – the high priests of this esoteric religion – intone litanies meaningless to those outside their faith. 'Lock off and cut. Stand by to roll-back and mix'. To most people they might just as well be speaking Latin, but there is no denying the power of their craft. Up on the main colour monitor, the one showing a picture that will eventually be seen by millions, the fantastic is taking place. A solid London police box is melting away into thin air.

'Oh, that's nothing,' dismisses one of the brethren, a skilled, long-serving member of the faith, basking in the title of Electronic

OVERLEAF:
Studio D at Lime Grove featuring Captain Maitland's ship from 'The Sensorites'.

17

Effects Designer. 'With this little gadget,' he says, pointing to a piece of wizardry identified simply as a 'Paint Box', 'You can treat the elements of any image as data in a computer's memory. The picture dots transpose as a bit pattern matrix in the memory. So, just as a computer program can move, resort and re-arrange conventional, digitised data, so the 'Paint Box' can process the elements of any picture image according to program.'

Simple? Yet the results are awe-inspiring. Using a device called a light-pen, which might just as well be termed a magician's wand, fragments from the monitor's picture are lifted, coloured, reshaped and transposed around the screen, like the pieces in a celestial jig-saw.

The 'Paint Box' is a standard tool of the television industry in the 1980s. However, had it been demonstrated to someone from the past, even from the scientifically enlightened Victorian age, the process would have appeared indistinguishable from magic.

And therein lies a clue to *Doctor Who*'s own brand of magic. With its glittering banks of high technology a television studio control room bears an uncanny resemblance to the Doctor's own example of super-science – the TARDIS.

Keeping pace with technology, the TARDIS console has changed with the passing of more than twenty years. So too has the design, complexity and sheer variety of equipment and facilities available to production crews working on the show. It is no exaggeration to say *Doctor Who* is one of the most technically demanding programmes being made anywhere in the world. Indeed its unique position as a showcase for developments within the industry often makes it an ideal platform for companies keen to show off their wares; witnessed in 1980 when a process called 'Scene-Synch' made its debut in the serial 'Meglos'. On the merits of its effectiveness in that story, the marketing company was able to negotiate a lucrative deal with the BBC for the use of Scene-Synch in a major drama production, *The Borgias*.

Such platforming is what keeps *Doctor Who* so often ahead of its rivals. Other productions may spend more money, and achieve slicker results, but after any significant episode run the end result is frequently a jaded, seen-it-all-before after-taste. *Doctor Who*'s gift is the constant allowance for freshness, change, and supreme inventiveness within its format. Only when those qualities are unavailable does the show ever suffer any real harm. Nowhere was this more evidenced than in 1985 with the decision to postpone production for eighteen months due to an inability to afford the very material and human resources *Doctor Who* needs to survive and flourish.

Pick any *Doctor Who* story at random and chances are it will require the following key personnel just at its planning stage:

A Producer to oversee the whole show; a writer to pen the script; a Script Editor to tailor the script exactly to the show's requirements; a Director in charge of tactically making the serial; a Production Designer to arrange the sets; a Costume Designer to look after wardrobe requirements; a Make-Up Designer to create the right 'look' for the artists; a Visual Effects Designer in charge

The TARDIS from 'The Keys of Marinus', coated in 'artex' and sprayed dark blue to give it an aged, battered look.

of all special hardware requirements; an Electronic Effects Designer to conjure up optical effects; a Special Sound recordist to devise background atmospherics, sound effects and special voices; an Incidental Music composer to write all the themes, links and stings; a Lighting Supervisor to give the right mood and look to the scenes; Film Cameramen; Sound Recordists and Editors to shoot location footage, and Studio Camera, Sound and Vision Supervisors to oversee 'interior' recording. All these just at the early production stages, long before teams of carpenters, seamstresses, freelance prop builders, casting agents and all the other supernumeraries of Television become involved. In all, a very lengthy and man-hour costly procedure.

To the uninitiated it probably appears miraculous that an episode should ever reach the screens at all, given that the fracturing of just one link – say a strike by scenery builders – can grind matters to an immediate halt. The 1979 serial 'Shada' is mute testament to Television's intrinsic fragility.

All the above demonstrates the current state of the craft by which *Doctor Who* is made. Given that as true, many an armchair intellectual might be tempted to muse, 'Surely it must have been a lot easier in the old days? All you needed was a good script, good actors, a few sets, and away you went. No problem . . .'

Such is the popular misconception about so-called 'old' Television, and frequently a cause why many, barring those nostalgic armchair intellectuals, tend to dismiss any idea of tuning into old programmes, taking refuge instead in a groan of despair whenever the legend (*repeat*) appears beside a TV guide programme listing. And even louder is the expectoration should the phrase (*black and white*) accompany it. That is Cardinal Sin Number One. 'If it's black and white, it's old and hence not worth watching. Far better another episode in a current soap opera than a creaking, 1964 episode of *Doctor Who*'. How often have such feelings as these been expressed in a household? The horns of a twin dilemma. Modern Television is flashy, not so well written, but eminently watchable; old Television may be better scripted, as rose-tinted memory is prone to serve, but pales behind the production standards of today.

Case closed. The Prosecution rests.

Is there a Defence? The answer: yes; but to prove it, and to put matters more in balance, requires an extended blinkering of perception thresholds, enough to accept a blending of the real with the fantastic. From the floor of the BBC television studios in West London this book is going to undertake a trip through time in that paragon of temporal engineering, the TARDIS.

It won't be a long voyage. In cosmic timescales it is doubtful the journey would even register. After all, what is twenty-five years to a science spanning all eternity in an infinity of space?

The sign outside the two swing doors says 'Studio 8'. The place is Television Centre, Wood Lane; the date, somewhere in the mid-1980s. Recording has just finished for a spell and many of the cast and crew have dispersed for dinner.

The studio itself is quite large, roughly two-thirds the size of a football pitch, ceilinged about as high as a church and populated by a multitude of lights, microphone booms, cameras, monitors and a few technicians. Several sets have been erected around the walls of the studio, one or two of which cover the main bulk of the floorspace. A glance through a script informs us that scenes shot on these sets today will be later edited into all four of the episodes comprising this story.

Standing to the side of a set is one of the five cameras used to shoot this episode. Sleek and compact, this white boxed machine, with its single, cowled lens, sits comfortably on a castored pedestal, the words *BBC TV COLOUR* emblazoned on the sides. The camera operator, a youngish man in jeans and an open-necked shirt, is studying a shooting script. Each page of the script is printed on coloured paper, the different colours denoting the episode for which any particular scene is destined: a blue page for an episode two scene, a pink page for an episode three scene, and so on.

At the operating end of the camera are series of buttons, dials and switches by which the cameraman can modify the image he is seeing through his viewfinder. Cables snake away from the camera and disappear through plug-points in the wall. These carry the electronic signals from the cameras up to monitors housed in the gallery control complex, a large, glass-fronted set of rooms, often referred to as 'The Fish Tank'. Here the Producer and Director control operations, assisted by their technical staff, including the Electronic Effects Designer with his bank of 'image processing' devices.

Our concern, however, is with just one artefact, currently standing alone and forgotten in one of the sets: the symbol of *Doctor Who*, the TARDIS.

A simple Yale key opens the door and at once, through the magic of television, we stand inside the Doctor's own control room. Brilliantly lit, the white walls are indented with ranks of shallow, circular depressions, punctuated by columned pillars at the corners. A single doorway leads off to the rest of the ship, and to the left of it is the wall frame housing the scanner.

Dominating the room's architecture is the control console, a hexagonal table of silvered panels inlaid with row after row, bank after bank of microswitches, LED displays, buttons and visual display units. All these centre towards the time rotor, a wedding cake-like structure encased within a polished glass cylinder.

Pushing a large, red lever closes the doors. The ship is sealed now and ready for flight. Flicking another switch raises the panel concealing the scanner. Linked to the TARDIS's telepathic circuits this scanner can show not only a view of the immediate outside but also, within limits, perspectives of other areas nearby.

H. G. Wells's legendary time-traveller remarked on the pulse-pounding excitement he felt as his hands first moved the lever to instigate his move through the fourth dimension's boundaries. The feeling is somewhat similar as unpractised fingers tentatively punch-out the code sequences needed for this 'short hop' flight. As the final sequence is entered, the room gives a slight lurch and a feeling, not unlike that experienced on a boat at sea, assails the senses. The previously muted background sound of the ship's hidden drive systems has changed in pitch from a low, meditative hum to a higher, more insistent thrumming. For better or for worse, the TARDIS is in flight.

Referencing the ship's instruction manual has revealed a procedure for pausing the craft's passage through time without actually occasioning it to land. Presumably this facility enabled the Lords of Gallifrey to snapshot selected timeframes in order to build up greater understanding of a world's evolution, without all the potential risks a landing would incur. Whatever the case, it is a facility eminently tailored to this voyage.

Operating the pause control slows the time rotor and steadies the image on the scanner. The date outside is revealed as 1980.

Immediately changes are apparent. The whole console has miraculously altered to a much simpler configuration of buttons and switches. The base underneath the control table is no longer conical in design but regulated into six squared panels. The time rotor too is different. Instead of the wedding-cake structure the glass column now encloses a single pillar into which brackets supporting neon-light tubes have been sunk. The TARDIS walls are the same but a double-door panel arrangement now frames the scanner screen.

The image presently on the screen is that of a tall, curly-haired individual. Swathed in a burgundy coat, an over-long scarf and a soft felt hat, the man's height lends him a commanding presence as he addresses a group of yellow-gowned aliens with up-swept coiffures. Moving beyond the set's perimeter, up into the 'Fish Tank', we can see on the master output monitor the rerun of a shot using 'The Quantel Unit', the pioneer of the image-processing devices which has just enabled a materialisation effect to be done during a tracking shot, something previously known to be impossible. Of 'Paint Box', however, there is no sign. It has yet to be made commercially available.

Dabbing the revised control switches moves us back another five years. This time, as vision once more stabilises, the changes are even more acute. To begin with, the console room is much smaller. The pillars at the wall corners have gone and so too has the single door through to the main part of the ship. The circled walls are still in evidence but the design is less regularised. Some walls feature large circular cut-outs, backed by a translucent material through which light is shining, other walls are solid with the circle patterns embossed. The console is, thankfully, the same but the colour-scheme has shifted from silver to a pale greenish-white.

Outside the TARDIS, its erstwhile owner is still in the same body, but dressed now in a short, red hacking jacket and grey trousers. The scarf is even more multi-coloured than its 1980 equivalent, giving the character a much more gypsy-like appearance.

A camera glides into view and a quick focus onto the script

The first *Radio Times* cover to feature *Doctor Who*, publicising the historical epic 'Marco Polo'.

24

**FEBRUARY 22—28**

Radio Times (Incorporating World Radio) February 20, 1964. Vol. 162: No. 2102.

# Radio Times

SIXPENCE

**BBC** **tv** **Sound**

## DR. WHO

The four travellers in time and space
return to Earth for a new adventure
beginning on Saturday in Television

**SEE PAGE 7**

•

## HUGH AND I

Laugh—with Terry Scott and Hugh Lloyd
as they resume their interrupted series in
Television on Saturday

**PAGE 9**

## BENNY HILL

Laugh—with the many Bennys in his new
show on Sunday afternoon in the Light

**PAGE 15**

## ERIC SYKES

Laugh—with him and Hattie Jacques as
they begin a series in Television on Tuesday

**PAGE 27**

**IN THE LIGHT AND
ON TELEVISION**

**World Heavyweight
Championship**

## SONNY LISTON
v.
## CASSIUS CLAY

SEE PAGE 29

•

**IN THE LIGHT**

The British, British Empire,
and European Championship

## HENRY COOPER
v.
## BRIAN LONDON

SEE PAGE 21

identifies the set as a 'Quarantine Area' – clearly not a place one would want to dwell for long. Before releasing the pause control again, though, two further facts are gleaned. Firstly 'Quantel' is not listed as part of the studio's manifest, and secondly, further examination of the script reveals far fewer coloured pages than before. The predominant colour is yellow, hinting that most of what will be shot today is destined for just one episode rather than the whole story.

Tumbling back five more years brings the date to Spring 1970. Curiously, and doubtless due to one of those paradoxes common to time-travel, the console is both inside our ship and outside in what appears to be a terrestial laboratory. Here a tall, elegantly dressed figure is hard at work on its innards while, nearby, a television is showing pictures of two space capsules docked in orbit. The console unit being worked on appears, at first glance, to be more robust than the version left behind in 1975. Certainly there are more controls, and suspicion grows that the overall diameter is wider than its temporal predecessor. A greater complexity of instrumentation is also detectable within the time rotor mechanism, but is is only when the penny finally drops that we realise the true nature of change is one of electrics over electronics. All the VDU teletext screens and LED display panels of the mid-Eighties' console have gone, replaced here by charge-actuated moving-coil dials, light bulb indicator lamps, large, hand-grip switches and arrays of very solid-looking levers.

As if in sympathy with this more cumbersome item of hardware the interior hum of the TARDIS is a lower, more sonorous sound than that left behind in the Eighties.

The studio environment seems much the same as before except that the shooting script is now completely uniform in colour. And closer examination of the front page reveals one extra detail: everything for episode one of this story is going to be recorded this session. Editing aside, by the time the cameras finish rolling tonight one complete episode will be 'in the can'.

At present, final rehearsals are under way. Above one of the main sets a huge blue screen has been draped, the purpose of which we discover on peeping into the gallery. Here the Director is liaising with a technician he refers to as 'The Inlay Operator' on the use of Colour Separation Overlay (CSO) for a scene. Using this technique one of the cameras aimed at the main set will be keyed not to see the colour blue. On the master output screen in the gallery the 'hole', created by the camera not being able to see blue, will be filled with the output from another camera, in this case a shot of an astronaut in space. The finished effect, the Director is assured, will be as if the actors on set are looking up at a giant television screen showing the image of an astronaut.

Once more we put the ship back into flight, but only for a brief moment. As the TARDIS crosses into the Nineteen-Sixties dramatic changes are instantly apparent.

The console room grows suddenly larger as other items of furniture start to appear – an old Sheraton chair, an ornate Chinese vase, even a battered old wooden clothes trunk. The scanner,

26

formerly part of the wall's architecture, is now visibly a TV monitor, hanging on gimbals from the roof. Some of the walls are as solid as ever, but others, amazingly, appear in our bemused gaze to be giant photographic blow-ups of the conventional, circular wall design.

Most disturbing of all, though, is the abrupt loss of colour perception. Everything has suddenly polarised into monochrome, replacing a full visual spectrum with all the intermediate shades of grey between black and white.

Turning our attention outside brings further shocks. The studio has shrunk. Where once the football pitch analogy applied, a tennis court comparison would now seem more apt. Even the ceiling is noticeably nearer the ground, lending the place a perceptibly more claustrophobic feel.

A figure darts into view, a rather shabbily-dressed little man in baggy check trousers and a shapeless old coat. He is followed by a camera, but not like ones seen in previous stop-overs. This machine has fewer electronic, and more manual, controls and there is a noted absence of the word 'COLOUR' from its markings. The logical conclusion that it must therefore be a simpler machine is balanced by the sobering observation that the camera's design is every bit as bulky, if not more so, than its 70s successors.

Visually, the biggest difference is at the picture-taking end of the camera. In place of the one, cowled lens, this version sports a turret of four projecting lenses, any one of which can be swivelled into place before the viewfinding/picture-taking apparatus.

Our journey is nearly accomplished as we pass by 1968 and head towards our landing point half a decade into the past. As the time rotor slows, the oft-quoted 'wheezing/groaning' sound of rematerialisation begins, audible now within the TARDIS control room. Lights flash on and off within the glass column as the whole internal mechanism begins to rotate on its own axis. The control room, vast now, with a glowing power unit hanging above the console is filled with the artefacts of the original Doctor – a food machine, the navigational computer banks, an eagle lectern and, in pride of place, a magnificent Ormolu clock.

The scanner, resting on its scaffold frame, shows a view of the studio beyond: six small, slightly cramped sets, a couple of large, shoe-shaped microphones on boom poles, four of the turret-fronted cameras, a host of studio floor staff, many of them in jackets, some even wearing ties . . .

As we move out of the TARDIS we notice the reason behind the imagined shrinking of the studio. It is not the same building. Stencilled lettering proclaims the venue as 'Studio D, Lime Grove', one of the BBC's other premises in West London, known in the Eighties more for news and current affairs broadcasting.

But this is not the 1980s. The calendar gives the year as 1963, an eventful time for Britain and the world. The Space Race is hotting up, the Cold War growing even colder. The Beatles are already embarked on their meteoric rise, and President Kennedy has still to fall. Ironically, the very day marking Kennedy's loss to the world will also see the public's introduction to *Doctor Who*.

Hardly the most fortunate of associations. *Doctor Who*'s launch at such a time of national shock and disbelief will be privately upsetting to many of those who have laboured long months preparing the series for transmission. In terms of technical accomplishment *Doctor Who* will mark something new and revolutionary from the BBC, and hopes for the series are very high. A lot of hard effort and enthusiasm has gone into its making, all of which could be threatened with undoing by events outside any programme scheduler's control . . .

Our time flight has brought us to the world of early Sixties BBC Television production to try and uncover the roots of *Doctor Who* that led to its first episode going out, ten minutes late, on Saturday 23 November, 1963. Then, as now, the production used the medium of television to the fullest, stretching the Corporation to the limits of technological capability. It deserved to survive the traumas of that November day, and survive it did, developing and progressing as it went along to become the backbone of Saturday night viewing on BBC Television.

In the public's eyes the beginning was November, but for others within the Corporation origins stretched back months beforehand, going beyond the first studio recording, beyond the designing of the TARDIS, predating any script-writing, or even the first allocations of production responsibility.

Before any of these could occur there had to be a spark . . .

# STRANGERS IN SPACE

ASSEMBLING THE jigsaw of *Doctor Who*'s conception draws pieces from three areas of the television industry.

Firstly, piecing together the BBC TV environment of the early Sixties shows why *Doctor Who* was not devised as a Children's Series. Often this tag has been applied to the programme, but never, ever, has it held a vestige of truth. In spite of being scheduled around the five o'clock timeslot, *Doctor Who* has always been a fully-fledged BBC Drama Series, made by the Drama Department in the same mould as *Z Cars*, *Adam Adamant Lives*, or, more recently, *Blake's 7* and *All Creatures Great and Small*.

Secondly, the ancestors of *Doctor Who* are worthy of note, especially considering the nature of the show. In Britain, more so than in other countries, science fiction has always had a stigma attached to it. Considering the technical complexities required, televised science fiction has frequently earned less than proportionately balanced critical response. The main body of audiences in the Sixties were adults who tended to regard TV sf as either children's fare, or as trash: an unfounded prejudice probably stemming from unwarranted comparisons with the comic-strip science fiction movie serials of the 1930s and 40s, or with the UK-banned 'horror' comics of the 1950s.

Thirdly, and most important of all in the genesis of *Doctor Who*, are the people who inspired it – the few who drew the notion of *Doctor Who* from the seeds of human inventiveness and put them down on paper. In this respect one name stands out. Strangely enough, for a series often stamped as more British than tea and crumpets, *Doctor Who*'s principal creator was not an Englishman, but a Canadian-born TV entrepreneur named Sydney Newman.

Newman not only inspired *Doctor Who*, he also played a major role in structuring the whole fabric of British television drama in the 1960s, adding considerably to the worldwide reputation for quality it still enjoys today.

While Television began in Britain during the 1930s, it was not until just after the Second World War that a regular broadcasting service commenced. This was BBC Television, an off-shoot of the world-renowned and world-respected BBC Radio service that had so admirably lived up to its motto to 'educate, inform and entertain' the general public throughout the war.

Although, by definition an entertainment industry, the BBC's status was more in common with a Civil Service Department than with the opportunistic realms of Theatre and Film. Class distinction and impeccable Home Counties accents were the orders of the day. Male presenters were expected to be black-tie-dressed while women wore evening gowns, and sometimes even tiaras.

In 1949 the world's first television science fiction production was broadcast by the BBC. Prophetically it was an adaptation of *The Time Machine* by H. G. Wells. It went out live as a one-part play from the studios at Alexandra Palace. It featured no film material, no exterior shooting and nothing whatsoever in the way of visual effects – such a department just did not exist in 1949.

At the helm was a Producer, although in addition to supervising the administrative side he was expected to liaise with the writer on the script and direct the play in the studio. His immediate staff were a Production Designer, responsible both for sets and prop building, and a Technical Manager to oversee setting up the studio equipment. Additionally there would have been a Wardrobe Mistress to arrange costuming, and a Make-up Lady to ensure no-one's nose gleamed under the studio lights.

Due to the state of television technology in 1949 no means of preserving this play existed. The electronic cameras captured the action, and powerful transmitters beamed the signals directly to the few homes in Britain equipped with television receivers. At that time the use of videotape to enable prerecording and editing was just a gleam of enthusiasm in the laboratory scientist's eye.

Four years later, in the summer of 1953, the BBC broadcast *The Quatermass Experiment*, a six part serial by Nigel Kneale, and a landmark as the first popularly accepted science fiction production. Again it was done live and so, from the cast's point-of-view, they were expected to learn their lines and movements as if they were doing a conventional four act stage play. Technically, however,

30

there had been two major and significant improvements.

The first was telecine. In the opening scenes of *The Quatermass Experiment* stock film library footage is used of a V2 rocket blasting off, coupled in with sub-orbital shots of the Earth's surface as seen from the stratosphere. These establishing sequences were on 16mm film. To insert them, or any other filmed material, required telecine transfer – literally the cine projection of the film onto a small screen being looked at by a television camera.

Telecine transfer was, and is, the responsibility of the studio Vision Mixer whose job is to switch the output picture (the one seen by the television audience) between the action on the studio floor and the scenes on film from the Telecine Department. Nowhere near as easy as it sounds, the trick is in the timing. Every sequence of film has a 'leader' strip which counts down in seconds from ten to the point where the action begins. Thus the Vision Mixer and the Director must time exactly when to begin running the leader in such a way that, as the scene on the studio floor finishes, the picture can be cut smoothly to the scene on film. Just a few seconds out either way in a live production can lead to a jump-in mid-scene or an embarrassed pause on the studio floor while the film is run up.

The second innovation to help *Quatermass* was telerecording. At first glance telerecording is the opposite of telecine; being a 16mm film camera shooting the image on a TV screen. This enabled the preservation of live programmes for subsequent retransmission or sale to other countries. The telerecording screen was exactly the same as a domestic television screen except that it was flat rather than curved, eliminating any distortion from the image when captured on film.

Production-wise, *The Quatermass Experiment* was the same as *The Time Machine*, save for two small, but significant additions. As the infected astronaut begins his terrible mutation into a plant life-form the BBC's Make-up people were required to devise 'half-stage' applications and appliances to give the creature a monsterish look. Finally, in the climax to episode five, the camera pans up the colonnades of Westminster Abbey to focus on the fully-grown alien monster, its fronds and tendrils twitching. In truth the TV realisation of Poet's Corner, Westminster Abbey was nothing more than a photographic blow-up, and the monster just the latex-coated hands of writer Nigel Kneale sticking out through a hole in the picture. But in historical retrospect it does count as a very early example of visual effects in a TV serial.

Two more *Quatermass* serials followed in 1955 and 1958 – respectively *Quatermass II* and *Quatermass and the Pit*. The former saw a move from Alexandra Palace to the BBC's new studios at Lime Grove which were bigger, and equipped with the new generation of videotape machines. Cumbersome and unwieldy, these record/playback devices did at least permit shows to be prerecorded in advance of transmission and allowed for a very crude form of editing.

In addition, the rudiments of a Visual Effects Department had been established to supply the serial's requirement for models and special props (space suits and gas-carrying meteorite pods). Special sound effects were still a problem though. The roar of a meteorite blazing through the air in *Quatermass II* still had to be accomplished by scratching a thumb-nail across a microphone mesh.

*Quatermass and the Pit* solved this headache by recourse to the infant Radiophonic Workshop – a special sounds' studio at the BBC's Delaware Road premises, geared to creating all manner of weird audio effects. They had begun life catering for the manic requirements of radio's *The Goon Show*, which stretched ingenuity to the full, requiring anything from Major Bloodnok's gastric eruptions to the sound of 'a batter pudding whizzing through the air, hitting a wall and slithering to the floor'.

Record audiences were attracted by *Quatermass and the Pit*, which regularly emptied pubs and clubs each Saturday night over its six week run. Not only was this good news for TV science

Sydney Newman, Head of BBC TV Drama in 1963 and the 'Godfather' of *Doctor Who*.

fiction it was also good news for the BBC, at a time when they were beginning to feel the effects of an increasingly powerful competitor – ITV.

Independent Television started in 1955. Instead of one large corporate body, like the BBC, ITV comprised a dozen or so smaller production companies, all making, and prerecording, programmes for sale to each other and overseas.

In planning this network of commercial stations the companies involved had unashamedly looked across the Atlantic in search of inspiration and blueprints. Unlike the BBC, which gleaned income from license money, ITV needed money from advertising, and tempting advertisers meant guaranteeing them ratings. Ergo, to get ratings it was absolutely vital that the ITV chiefs broadcast programmes geared to attract a maximum audience. Thus a careful analysis of the USA system was undertaken in the belief that no race under the sun knew how to sell products as well as Americans.

The ITV policy of bringing a transatlantic style to British Television extended far beyond merely an emulation of programming. Not only did ITV want concepts, they also wanted expertise, and that determined an import drive.

Enter Toronto-born Sydney Newman. Qualified in painting, drawing and commercial art, Newman joined the National Film Board of Canada as a Producer in 1947, having previously worked in Hollywood from 1938. Between 1947 and 1952 he produced no less than 300 short films, many of them for the Canadian Government, and on these merits he was appointed Director of Outside Broadcasts, Features and Documentaries with the Canadian Broadcasting Corporation in 1952.

By 1958 Newman was the Drama Supervisor for CBC and was producing the very successful Canadian Television Theatre presentations when he was approached by the ABC TV company in England (now London Weekend Television). They had

witnessed, and were very impressed with, Newman's fresh approach to TV Drama. His influence at CBC had brought a new generation of writers, Directors and actors into the medium, all geared towards making drama appeal to mass audiences.

Newman had realised that, because of cultural inequalities, many people were not ardent followers of drama as presented in the Theatre. They were, however, more inclined to be cinema-goers. Hence the brief he handed out to his staff was to make TV drama a popular medium, like the cinema, by having it comment and reflect on worlds and situations familiar to mass audiences. He set high standards for writers and Directors, but his over-riding dictate was that televised drama should make plain statements, falsified neither by sentiment nor by doctrinaire belief. In other words, 'kitchen sink' drama that was easy to understand and sympathise with.

ABC TV wanted Newman to bring these same qualities to England, and offered him a post in control of their series *Armchair Theatre*. Newman accepted, not so much for financial reasons but because he found England, with its more polarised divisions of class and attitude, an irresistible challenge. Could his same notion of 'agitational contemporaneity' work for *Armchair Theatre* as it had worked for North American TV drama?

The results spoke for themselves. Under BBC-trained Producer Dennis Vance, *Armchair Theatre* achieved a modest success. Under the helm of Sydney Newman, the weekly productions scored in the top ten ratings chart for a staggering thirty-two out of thirty-seven weeks between Autumn 1959 and Summer 1960, with audiences averaging upwards of 12 million.

As well as *Armchair Theatre*, Sydney Newman is most remembered, at ABC, for his other hit TV show, *The Avengers*. Conceived initially as a spy series for Ian Hendry and Patrick MacNee, *The Avengers* quickly developed into a stylish combination of James Bond action/adventure with frequent science fiction overtones, the latter a narrative form much loved by Newman.

On that basis, and almost forgotten between these two dramatic giants, Newman commissioned and produced a science fiction serial for children in 1959 called *Pathfinders in Space*, a serial in seven parts, penned by Eric Paice and Malcolm Hulke – two authors who shared a friend in fellow writer David Whitaker, of whom more will be discussed in later chapters.

In his book *With an Independent Air* Howard Thomas, a contemporary of Sydney Newman at ABC TV, insists the idea of *Doctor Who* was dreamed up by Newman, while he was still at ITV, only to have the idea rejected by the sanctioning board. In a letter replying to these allegations, Newman is very adamant this was not the case, insisting instead that Thomas was confusing *Doctor Who* with the *Pathfinders* series.

Such a misconception is easy to understand. Of all the science fiction programmes screened on British Television none is so close an ancestor to *Doctor Who* as *Pathfinders*.

*Pathfinders in Space* obeyed all the ground rules Sydney

Newman laid down for doing drama on Television. Unlike the *Quatermass* productions, which although technically similar to *Doctor Who* were more thriller serials with fantastic overtones, *Pathfinders* was definitive science fiction. It extemporised on man's quest into space (a very popular talking point in the post-Sputnik Fifties), tackling the problems realistically with a strict observance of scientific laws. The higher, more metaphysical elements of literary space fiction were avoided, keeping the whole series fast moving and thus more likely to pick up good audiences – despite the British public's general anathema to sf around that period.

The ploy worked and from its modest slot around 4.30 on Sunday afternoons *Pathfinders in Space* attracted the first real family audience for a science fiction serial.

*Pathfinders in Space* concerns the events surrounding an early attempt to blaze a trail into space by a small group of British explorers. Professor Wedgewood (Peter Williams) leads the first team and is successfully launched into space. His supply rocket, however, cannot take off automatically and so his children, Valerie, Geoffrey and Jimmy volunteer to save the expedition. After their ship is in space they find a stowaway, and as the two rockets continue their journey into deep space, a third rocket appears . . . a spaceship from nowhere. Professor Wedgewood's rocket lands on the Moon and the supply rocket, brought by his children, lands some 150 miles away. Wedgewood sets out to find it and both parties discover that someone has already arrived on the Moon before them . . .

The three children find a cave containing relics of a previous civilisation. Professor Wedgewood also finds proof of a landing in the distant past and now wonders whether the alien spacecraft will reveal its secrets. Eventually the two parties meet up and commence searching inside the ancient craft. As they do so, meteorites begin bombarding the Moon. Disaster strikes the explorers and Wedgewood is faced with a terrible decision. One of the rockets has been destroyed and it is decided only Valerie and one other member of the group can return home, leaving perhaps no hope of rescue for the others. But maybe there is one other, but risky, alternative: the mystery spaceship . . .

This first serial, grandiose as its plot sounds, was a live production, not even telerecorded for posterity due to cost factors. In a way, this was perhaps just as well. Gerald Flood, co-starring as astronaut pilot Conway Henderson, remembers clearly a panic in the studio control room when it was realised that another character, dressed in full space suit, was inaudible to the microphones once he had latched down his space helmet.

Regardless of technical hitches *Pathfinders in Space* was judged a great success, leading to a second series being commissioned in 1960.

This was *Pathfinders to Mars*, a six-episode production, again by Messrs Hulke and Paice, which opted for prerecording in a bid to retain the sanity of Director Guy Verney. Peter Williams once more played the all-wise Professor Wedgewood while Gerald Flood returned as the square-jawed hero Conway Henderson.

Significantly though a new character was introduced, Harcourt Brown, a tetchy, cantankerous scientist of mysterious background, compellingly played by George Coulouris.

Keen to encourage a wider audience, Sydney Newman, as Producer, also cast a female lead in the series to play the part of Professor Meadows, an 'older woman' character who could relate the plot's weird happenings in human terms to the young, but now more grown-up, children.

In *Pathfinders to Mars*, Brown, an imposter aboard the latest interplanetary rocket launch, deliberately sabotages the flight, causing the rocket to make an emergency landing on Mars. This affords Brown a chance to explore the planet which he believes not to be as dead as it first appears. His assumption is correct. The Martian encampment they find may be deserted but the lichen-like vegetation, triggered into accelerated growth by a light drizzle of rain, proves more than just a minor hazard for the astronauts as they race against time to repair the ship.

By the end of the serial, Harcourt Brown, who begins as a very sinister type, has evolved into a more whimsical, if somewhat selfish, personality, prone to romancing about a trip to Venus.

As if in answer to this prayer one further *Pathfinders* production was launched in 1961 – the most ambitious to date, *Pathfinders to Venus*. Shot in eight episodes, this serial, again from the Newman/Paice/Hulke/Verney team, included an extra name on the credits – Derek Freeborn, responsible for the very demanding Visual Effects, including working model rockets, a fight between two dinosaurs, a miniature Venusian city and, just for good measure, an erupting volcano.

The relative complexity of the Visual Effects required a far greater use of filmed inserts. Excessive editing of videotape was not to be encouraged in 1961 and so Newman worked to the formula of having live action done in the electronic studio, and the Visual Effects, plus other control critical sequences, done on film – a small, but important development in British science fiction programme making.

The *Pathfinders* series proved a popular audience winner, like much of Newman's drama output. Indeed, so popular were the *Pathfinders* characters that several of them were hived off to appear in another children's sf serial, *City Beneath the Sea*, a well written technological thriller penned by John Lucarotti.

In 1960, Hugh Greene, a member of the Board of Governors at the BBC, had abruptly dismissed the claim that ITV was as much a public service body as the BBC, cynically despatching its press tag as 'the people's Television'. Yet it was clear by 1962 that the Corporation was lagging badly behind, not only with ratings but with styles of dramatic presentation. ITV, with *Pathfinders* and Gerry Anderson's *Fireball XL5* had advanced the techniques of Television for younger audiences. BBC, by contrast, still offered Dickensian classics as staple fare to growing legions of space age children. Something needed to be done.

The opportunity arose when Michael Barry, the BBC's long-standing Head of Drama, resigned in 1961 to join the new Irish

The plot synopses for Sydney Newman's *Pathfinders* series, in many respects the ancestor of *Doctor Who*.

36

# PATHFINDERS IN SPACE

## A SERIAL IN 7 PARTS
by MALCOLM HULKE and ERIC PAICE

starring    PETER WILLIAMS

HAROLD GOLDBLATT    GERALD FLOOD

Produced by          SIDNEY NEWMAN

Directed by          GUY VERNEY

Episode 1    CONVOY TO THE MOON

Episode 2    SPACESHIP FROM NOWHERE

Episode 3    LUNA BRIDGEHEAD

Episode 4    THE MAN IN THE MOON

Episode 5    THE WORLD OF LOST TOYS

Episode 6    DISASTER ON THE MOON

Episode 7    RESCUE IN SPACE

Professor Wedgwood leads the first team of Moon explorers and is successfully launched into space. His supply rocket, however, cannot take off by automatic pilot and his children, Valerie, Geoffrey and Jimmy volunteer to save the expedition. After their ship is in space they find a stowaway. The two rockets continue their journey into deep space and, as they near the moon, a third rocket appears.... a spaceship from nowhere. Professor Wedgwood's rocket lands on the moon and the supply rocket, brought by his children, lands some 150 miles away. Wedgwood sets out to find it and both parties discover that someone had already landed on the moon before them. The three children find a cave containing relics of a previous civilisation then make another startling discovery. Professor Wedgwood also finds proof of a landing in the distant past and now wonders whether the alien spaceship will reveal its secrets. The two parties meet up and the Professor and his children explore inside an ancient spaceship. As they do so, meteorites are bombarding the moon. Disaster strikes the explorers and Wedgwood is faced with a terrible decision. One of their rockets is destroyed by the meteorites and it is decided that only Valerie and another of their party can return to Earth. Then Professor Wedgwood makes a daring bid for safety....

A science-fiction series for children in seven 30 minute episodes distributed by:-
ASSOCIATED BRITISH-PATHE LTD.          2 Dean Street, London W. 1.
Telephone: GERrard 0444                 Cables: PATHIREMA

---

# PATHFINDERS TO MARS

## A SERIAL IN 6 EPISODES
by MALCOLM HULKE and ERIC PAICE

### Starring

Peter Williams as Professor Wedgwood

George Coulouis as The Impostor

Gerald Flood as Conway Henderson

Designed by DAVID GILLESPIE

Programme Adviser MARY FIELD

Producer SYDNEY NEWMAN

Directed by GUY VERNEY

Conway Henderson, the scientific journalist, consents to pilot a new interstellar rocket. Young Geoffrey Wedgwood will be one of the crew, and Henderson's niece Margaret - due for a holiday with her uncle - persuades him to take her, too. Meanwhile the place of Professor Dyson, is taken by an unidentified man believed by Wedgwood and the rocket crew to be Dyson.

The imposter, Brown, sabotages the rocket's radio receiver, so that Henderson and the rest of the crew cannot be told of his real identity. He is in touch with a mysterious "Sector Ten", which has apparently planned his actions. Henderson locates the rocket's supply capsules in orbit around the moon - but while he and the crew are unloading, Brown manages to get control of the rocket - and to hold Margaret as hostage.

---

# PATHFINDERS TO VENUS

## A SERIAL IN 8 EPISODES
by MALCOLM HULKE and ERIC PAICE

### Starring

George Coulouris as Harcourt Brown

Gerald Flood as Conway Henderson

Graydon Gould as Captain Wilson

Designed by DAVID GILLESPIE  Special Effects DEREK FREEBORN  Programme Adviser MARY FIELD

Producer SYDNEY NEWMAN  Directed by GUY VERNEY

Returning from their visit to Mars, the crew of the British space-ship M.R.4. intercepts a distress signal from a rocket in orbit around Venus. Manned by American astronaut, Wilson, it has been struck by a meteor, and is fast running out of oxygen. Wilson warns M.R.4. that his instruments have gone out of action and soon M.R.4. begins to react in a similar way. Only prompt action by the pilot, Henderson saves it from disaster. Brown - a science-fiction writer on board M.R.4. fakes a message so that Henderson believes the American has been forced to land on Venus.

M.R.4. lands safely in the depths of a thick forest. Henderson, Professor Meadows and Brown prepare to comb the forest for the American. Geoff and Margaret are left alone, and Geoff sees the American's space-ship on radar: it is coming in to land. It lands nearby: but when Geoff and Margaret reach it, the astronaut has vanished, and his cabin has been torn apart by some creature with enormous strength.

The children make radio contact with the rest who are still exploring the forest of Venus. On their way back, Brown suddenly disappears and later finds himself beside the Astronaut, Wilson; they have both been carried unconscious, to the edge of the forest facing a range of hills. Brown insists that behind the hills is a city built by the inhabitants of Venus, and they decide to try to reach it. Margaret and Professor Meadows, in the empty British space-ship, shut themselves in the control cabin when they see a hairy hand trying to force an entrance. Then Henderson too, disappears.

television network, Telefís Éireann in Dublin. After some debate, the BBC swallowed its pride and offered the post to Sydney Newman.

Newman accepted the job, even though it meant taking a drop in salary. For him, compensation lay in taking control over the entire, vast dramatic output of the BBC, with almost unlimited executive powers to restructure it as he saw fit.

Almost Newman's first act at the BBC was to decimate the existing Script Department under Donald Wilson. This unit had been set up originally to refine the art of specific writing for Television; either by seeking out works of literature suitable for adaption, or by commissioning new material and applying it to the 'TV-writing art form'. The predominant over-view in this Department was that Television held a special kind of mystique; that writing and producing drama for it demanded special levels of skill which were to be somewhere between the scopes of the Theatre and the Cinema.

Newman immediately judged this department to be an out-of-date dinosaur, so it was abolished. In its place, Newman substituted three departments: Plays, Series, and Serials.

Plays handled just that: single one-off productions including, strangely enough, opera, which was felt owed more to drama than to music.

Series were deemed to be longer plays, broken down into episodes for convenience of presentation. They would be more inclined *not* to end on cliff-hangers.

Serials were judged to be weekly productions, often year-round in production, that would always end on a note prompting the viewer to tune in again next week to watch the continuation. Existing examples at that time were *Compact* and *Starr and Company*.

A revised production hierarchy was also instigated by Sydney Newman, again modelled on the American system adopted by ABC. Before, as typified by Rudolph Cartier on the *Quatermass* shows, a Producer was expected both to produce, direct and, to an extent, liaise, with the writer on his script content. Under the Newman system, each Producer would be allocated a Story (Script) Editor to free him from writing overheads, and a pool of (mostly staff) Directors actually to make the programmes. The Producer would still be in overall charge, but his or her role was now far more strategic than tactical.

By Spring 1963, the groundwork of restructuring the BBC had been done. The big task now was to take on ITV – and win – which is where *Doctor Who* entered the scene. Sydney Newman takes up the story:

'As Head of the Drama Group, I was privy to problems of scheduling. Probably articulated by Donald Baverstock, Controller of BBC 1 or Stuart Hood, Controller of Programmes, there was a gap in the ratings on Saturday afternoons between BBC's vastly popular sports coverage, ending at 5.15, and the start at 5.45 of an equally popular pop music programme [*Juke Box Jury*]. What was

between them was, I vaguely recall, a children's classic drama serial, i.e. Charles Dickens dramatisations etc. This could be moved to Sunday if the Drama Department could come up with something more suitable.

'So, we required a new programme that would bridge the state of mind of sports fans, and the teenage pop music audience, while attracting and holding the children's audience accustomed to their Saturday afternoon serial. So that's the "why" of *Doctor Who*.

'The problem was, as I saw it, that it had to be a children's programme and still attract adults and teenagers. And also, as a children's programme, I was intent upon it containing basic factual information that could be described as educational – or, at least, mind-opening for them.

'So my first thought was of a time-space machine (thanks to H. G. Wells) in which contemporary characters (one of whom I wanted to be a 12-13 year old) would be able to travel forward and backward in time, and inward and outward in space. All stories were to be based on scientific and historical facts as we knew them at that time.

'Space also meant outer space, intergalactic travel, but again based on understood fact. So no bug-eyed monsters which I had always thought to be the cheapest form of science fiction.

'Re time. How wonderful, I thought, if today's humans could find themselves on the shores of England seeing and getting mixed up with Caesar's army in 54 BC, landing to take over the country; be in burning Rome as Nero fiddled; get involved in Europe's tragic thirty years war, etc., etc.

'That was the scheme, so how to dress it up?

'One thing I was certain of. The space-time machine had to be a very pedestrian-looking, everyday object to shock audiences into not taking the world around them for granted. It must be vast inside but small outside.

'Well, how did it get to be on Earth? Who would run it?

'To answer both questions I dreamed up the character of a man who is 764 years old; who is senile but with extraordinary flashes of intellectual brilliance. A crotchety old bugger (any kid's grandfather) who had, in a state of terror, escaped in his machine from an advanced civilisation on a distant planet which had been taken over by some unknown enemy. He didn't know who he was anymore, and neither did the Earthlings, hence his name, Doctor Who; he didn't know precisely where his home was; he did not fully know how to operate the time-space machine.

'In short, he never intended to come to our Earth. In trying to go home he simply pressed the wrong buttons – and kept on pressing the wrong buttons, taking his human passengers backwards and forwards, and in and out of time and space.

'I also felt that no serial/story should last longer than between four and six episodes (I didn't want to risk losing audiences for longer, should one story not appeal). Each episode had to end with a cliff-hanger and repeat this at the start of the next episode.

'I believe I put the above into a memo addressed to Donald Wilson whom I had appointed as my Head of Serials. I called him into my office, handed my memo to him and immodestly said, "Here's a great idea for Saturday afternoons. What do you think?"

'Donald perused it, looked up at me, scratched his head, grinned, and said, "Not bad. Maybe." Donald was a very cautious Scot, but his "maybe" was right. A lot of ideas can really go to hell in production; writing, casting, direction all being uncertain variables.

'When, some time later, he and I discussed who might take over the responsibility for producing it I rejected the traditional drama types, who did the children's serials, and said that I wanted somebody, full of vinegar, who'd be prepared to break rules in doing the show. Somebody young with a sense of "today" – the early "Swinging London" days.

'I phoned Verity Lambert, who had been on my *Armchair Theatre* staff at ABC. She had never directed, produced, acted or written drama – but, by God, she was a bright, highly intelligent, outspoken Production Secretary who took no nonsense and never gave any – but all with winning charm. I offered her the job and after Donald Wilson met her she joined us. I have a vague recollection that Donald Wilson at first sniffed at Verity Lambert's "independent" ways. Knowing both of them, I knew they would hit it off when they got to know one another better. They did.'

By early 1963 the stage for *Doctor Who* was set. Through *Quatermass* and *Pathfinders* it had been proved that the somewhat eclectic medium of science fiction could be transposed into popular television entertainment. Especially in the case of *Pathfinders*, its strength had drawn from a balance of well rounded characters in situations still identifiable to the viewers: Newman's drive for plain statements.

Technology, too, had reached a point where Producers, working in electronic studio environments, needed to fear no longer the pitfalls of live television. Prerecording was possible; so too were a range of optical and mechanical visual effects denied to the makers of *The Time Machine* and *The Quatermass Experiment*.

Finally, the working hierarchy was now available to make real Newman's dream of a long-running science fiction serial. Debutting Producer Verity Lambert would have access to a pool of new and established Directors physically to make the shows, plus, in the office next door, her most valued asset of all – a resident Script-Editor.

Normally in the commissioning of a series, both Producer and Script-Editor are appointed virtually simultaneously. However, because of the steps involved in bringing Verity Lambert over from ABC, *Doctor Who* gained its father long before it found its mother. In the beginning was the Script-Editor.

# THE DALEKS

The Cusick Stories
Serial 'B'

**Synopsis:** For Ian and Barbara, the hasty flight from freezing Paleolithic Earth has brought them no nearer a return to the comforts of England in 1963. Stepping from the uncertain sanctuary of the TARDIS, an even more forbidding landscape awaits them – a forest of whitened, petrified trees, soil turned to ash, and everywhere a deathly hush. The Doctor tells them they have left Earth completely and are now out far beyond the Solar System. His initial prognosis, that the planet is totally dead, is backed up by all they see, even when the four surmount a ridge and see, in the valley below, the gleaming spires of a deserted, metal city.

The Doctor wants to explore, but the two teachers say no. All manner of dangers could lie down there, and only the Doctor knows how to operate the ship. However the wily old man gets his way, surreptitiously sabotaging the TARDIS to make it look like mechanical failure, and suggesting the city as the only source of repair.

Once in the city the time-travellers find it far from dead.

OVERLEAF:
The Dalek city as seen by the film camera; a wreath of dry ice enshrouds the model.

41

Hideously scarred mutants in metal machines – the survivors of a terrible thermonuclear war – capture and imprison them, believing the four to be Thals, the other race on this planet whom these Daleks once fought.

Sent back into the forest to fetch medicine from the TARDIS, Susan encounters one of the Thals. He and his people are in need of food, and a party has been sent here to investigate the Dalek city.

The Daleks establish contact with the Thals and promise them food, but it is a trap. Their intention is extermination only. The travellers escape and manage to warn the Thal party in time to save most of them. Back in the forest the Doctor discovers the Daleks have taken the piece he sabotaged from the TARDIS. Without it they are stranded here forever.

Gradually they enlist the help of the Thals, persuading them to overcome their pacifist lifestyle and to fight for their share of this planet. The struggle must be carried back to the Dalek city, they argue. Eventually a two-pronged attack is agreed on. Ian and Barbara will lead a small expedition into the city from the rear, while the larger group creates a diversion.

The trek proves long and arduous, with casualties mounting as they forge through swamps and mountains before finally breaking into the Dalek city.

Fighting begins when they learn the Daleks intend to pollute the atmosphere with even more radioactive fallout, which will kill the Thals. Dalek firepower threatens to destroy the expeditionary force until the attackers hit on the idea of disabling the city's power generators. With no static electricity coming through the floor the Dalek machines fail, killing their occupants inside. The planet now belongs to the Thals . . .

Recovering the fluid link device from the TARDIS the time-travellers set off once more. But no sooner have they dematerialised than an explosion rocks the ship . . .

**Background:** Quite simply, this was the story which launched *Doctor Who*. Ratings and audience appreciation for the first serial, 'The Tribe of Gum', were good, and indeed above the average for BBC's Children's broadcasting. It had done better than the 5.30 Sunday Classic Serial and had proved an effective challenge to ITV's Saturday afternoon serial, *The Buccaneers*. 'The Daleks', however, took the show up into the rarified heights of peak viewing, prompting programme schedulers to see it as a very useful keystone in grabbing audiences for the whole of Saturday evening – which had been Donald Baverstock's prime intention all along.

Part One takes the greatest credit for hooking its audiences. Oddly enough, production problems first time around on this episode, 'The Dead Planet', occasioned it to be completely remounted and rerecorded between Episodes Three and Four, the only time this has happened in *Doctor Who*'s entire history aside from the remount of the pilot (see Chapter Three).

This put *Doctor Who*'s recording schedules back by one week,

OPPOSITE:
Susan (Carole Ann Ford) and the Thal Queen, Dyoni (Virginia Wetherell).

OVERLEAF:
The blueprints for the Magnedon, the metal monster discovered by the TARDIS crew on Skaro, and the crystalline flower found by Susan in the petrified forest there.

44

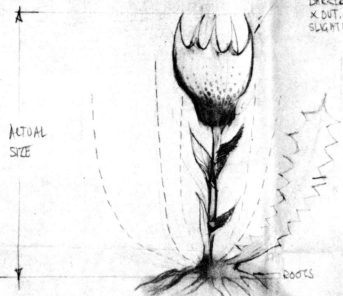

PLANT MADE OF SUGAR
OR CONFECTIONARY RATHER
PALE PINK IN COLOUR WITH
DARKER PINK DOTS INSIDE
X OUT. MUST CRUMBLE WHEN
SLIGHTLY PRESSED.

ACTUAL
SIZE

CACTCUS TYPE
LEAVES
ABOUT 6 TO 8 LEAVES
OF SOME SUBSTANTIAL
MATERIAL
RATHER FADED GREEN
IN COLOUR

ROOTS

PLANTS — 4/OFF

| CONSTRUCTION | PAINTERS | ARTISTS |
| --- | --- | --- |

AS ABOVE X DISCUSSION

OF MONSTER X FLOWER.

3'-9" APPROX.

SPIKES

EYES ON STALKS
PUT GLASS IN.

1'-10" APPROX

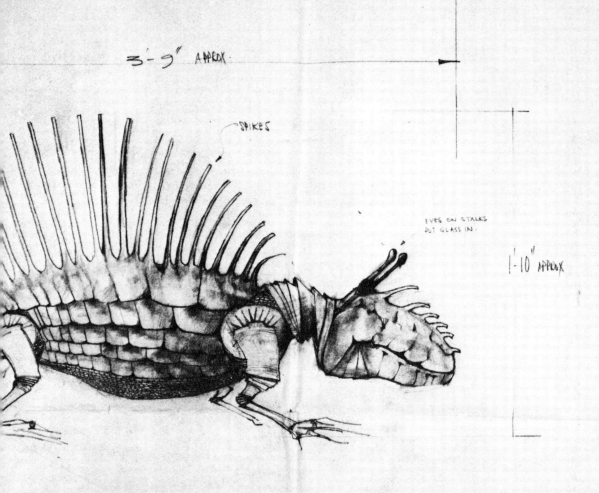

TO LOOK AS IF MADE OF METAL, COULD BE MADE OF PLASTER OVER
E X COVERED WITH TIN PLATES & METAL FOIL, FINISH. AGED PEWTER IN GENERAL APPEARANCE.
    OR A GOOD MATERIAL TO USE IS:— "SISALATION"
                    'COPPER SURFACED SISAL KRAFT PAPER'
                    FROM:—
                    J.H. SANKEY & SONS LTD.
                    ESSEX WORKS.
                    RIPPLE ROAD.
                    BARKING.
                    ESSEX.

— 1/OFF.

STOCK

BBC tv   DESIGN DEPARTMENT

SHEET NO.                    DATE DRAWN
NO. OF SHEETS               SCALE

DISTRIBUTION

| | | |
|---|---|---|
| ALLOCATIONS | DESIGNER EALING 1 | PRODUCER |
| A.P.M. (TEL) | DESIGN ORGANISER 2 | SCENE MASTER |
| BACK PROJECTION | DRAPES | ASST. SCENEMASTER |
| GRAPHICS | ELECTRICIANS | SCENERY STORES |
| CARPENTERS | ESTIMATOR | SCENIC ARTISTS |
| CON. MANAGER | P.M'S OFFICE 2 | SPECIAL EFFECTS |
| DESIGNER | METAL WORKERS | SUPPLY FOREMAN |
| DESIGN ASST. | PAINTERS | SUPPLY ORGANISER |
| TONY REEVES | VERITY LAMBERT | TONY FOSTER |

ESTIMATOR                PRODUCER CHRIS BARRY
                         DESIGNER RAYMOND P CUSICK EXT 2563
                         DRAWN BY
DATE 31-10-63            ZERO DATE 13/11/63   V.T.R. DATE 15/11/63
A.D.G.                   FILM DATE        TRANS. DATE
                         PRODUCTION
DATE 2/11/63            DR. WHO Nº1 SERIES B
STUDIO D. L/G.

but few would deny the worth of having done it. Layering suspense element upon suspense element, the episode builds up tension almost to breaking point as audiences ponder the big question: 'What lives in that city?' The final 'sting', as Barbara emerges from the lift and screams in terror at the approach of . . . something, stands as one of the finest cliff-hangers any serial has ever boasted. According to Terry Nation, after 'The Dead Planet' went out, he was deluged with phone calls from friends and colleagues, all wanting to know, 'What was it?' Just what was the object of Barbara's terror that viewers had only seen so far as a suction cup visible through a circular lens cowl?

The Dalek machines provided the answer a week later. With an unhuman shape, gliding motion, array of gadgets and grating voice, their fame spread, by word of mouth, like wild-fire throughout the schools of Britain. They were unlike anything ever seen before and for a while even the term 'Dalek Operator', credited at the end of each episode, substantiated the myth that they were actually radio-controlled robots.

Part of the fascination lay in the mystery of what exactly lurked inside the casings. Going on the Cinema's maxim about what you imagine you'll see often being more frightening than what you actually do see, the production team on 'The Daleks' chose wisely not to show the mutants inside the casings, save by suggestion and the odd teaser.

AFM Michael Ferguson played the Dalek claw seen at the end of episode four, but although convincing to the audience, this claw was nothing more elaborate than a joke shop gorilla hand covered in grease.

Only once was the full 'adult' Dalek mutant paraded in public. Interviewed by, of all newspapers, *The Daily Worker* (now *The Morning Star*), Raymond Cusick provided them with a colour illustration interpreting his idea of what lay inside. But such was the circulation of *The Daily Worker* in 1963 that few of *Doctor Who*'s growing army of fans ever saw it.

## Production Credits

Serial 'B'
Seven Episodes
Black and White

| | |
|---|---|
| 'The Dead Planet' | 21 December 1963 |
| 'The Survivors' | 28 December 1963 |
| 'The Escape' | 4 January 1964 |
| 'The Ambush' | 11 January 1964 |
| 'The Expedition' | 18 January 1964 |
| 'The Ordeal' | 25 January 1964 |
| 'The Rescue' | 1 February 1964 |

### Cast

| | |
|---|---|
| Doctor Who | William Hartnell |
| Ian Chesterton | William Russell |
| Barbara Wright | Jacqueline Hill |
| Susan Foreman | Carole Ann Ford |
| | |
| Alydon | John Lee |
| Ganatus | Philip Bond |
| Dyoni | Virginia Wetherell |
| Temmosus | Alan Wheatley |
| Elyon | Gerald Curtis |
| Kristas | Jonathan Crane |
| Antodus | Marcus Hammond |
| Other Thals | Chris Browning, Katie Cashfield, Vez Delahunt, Kevin Glenny, Ruth Harrison, Lesley Hill, Steve Pokol, Jeanette Rossini, Eric Smith |
| Dalek Voices | Peter Hawkins |
| | David Graham |
| Daleks | Robert Jewell, Kevin Manser, Michael Summerton, Gerald Taylor, Peter Murphy |

### Crew

| | |
|---|---|
| Production Assistant | Norman Stewart |
| Assistant Floor Manager | Michael Ferguson |
| Costume Supervisor | Daphne Dare |
| Make-up Supervisor | Elizabeth Blattner |
| Incidental Music | Tristram Cary |
| Story Editor | David Whitaker |
| Designer | Raymond Cusick |
| Designer (6) | Jeremy Davies |
| Associate Producer | Mervyn Pinfield |
| Producer | Verity Lambert |
| Director (1, 2, 4, 5) | Christopher Barry |
| Director (1, 6, 7) | Richard Martin |

# THE EDGE OF DESTRUCTION

The Cusick Stories
Serial 'C'

OVERLEAF:
An extract from the camera
script of 'The Edge of
Destruction' by David
Whitaker; reproduced by
permission of the BBC and
David Whitaker's Estate.

**Synopsis:** A mystery explosion has trapped the four time-travellers inside the TARDIS. Plunged into near darkness, none of the control systems are working, leaving the craft, to all intents and purposes, hanging dead in space.

The aftermath of the explosion has left all four companions suffering various degrees of concussion, states of mind leading tempers and suspicions all round to rise in the silent, shadow-filled atmosphere of the dormant craft.

Recovering gradually, the travellers find it impossible to re-activate the TARDIS's flight systems, and even machinery that supplies food and drink, though still in action, registers 'Empty'. The scanner is showing strange pictures that bear no resemblance to what is outside. The doors open and shut on their own, and beyond them is nothing but the void of space.

The Doctor is sceptical of the explanations offered by his companions. Susan and Barbara fear some alien intelligence has invaded the ship; Ian is more practical and is convinced there is simply a technical fault. With no-one yet fully recovered, and as

51

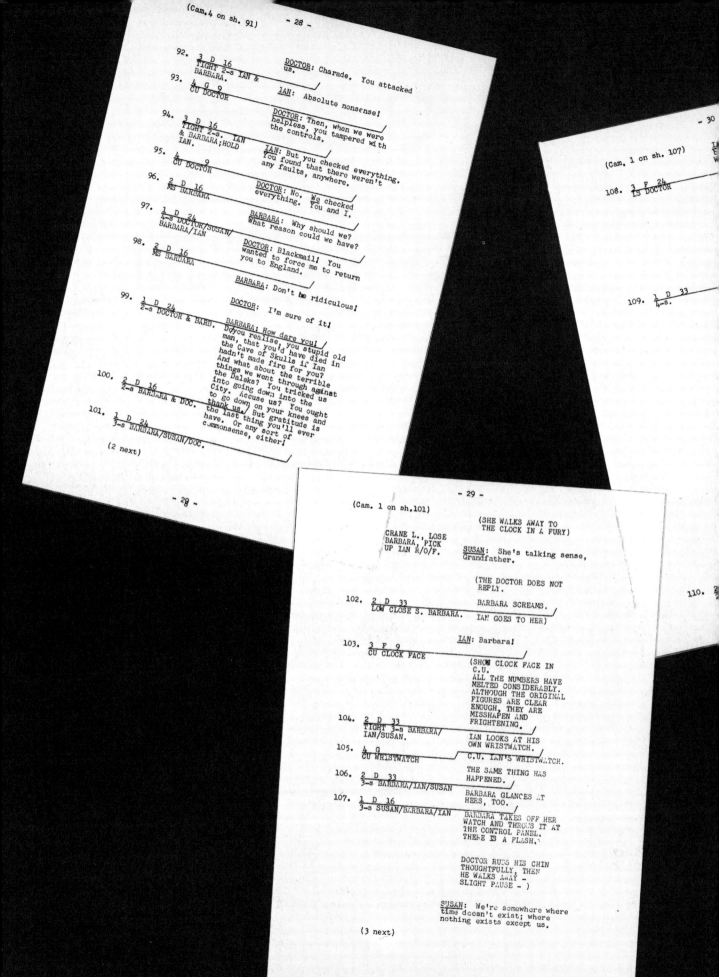

92. 3 D 16    DOCTOR: Charade. You attacked
TIGHT 2-s IAN &    us.
BARBARA.

93. 4 G 9    IAN: Absolute nonsense!
CU DOCTOR

94. 3 D 16    DOCTOR: Then, when we were
TIGHT 2-s. IAN    helpless, you tampered with
& BARBARA;HOLD    the controls.
IAN.

IAN: But you checked everything.
95. 4 9    You found that there weren't
CU DOCTOR    any faults, anywhere.

96. 2 D 16    DOCTOR: No. We checked
MS BARBARA    everything. You and I,

97. 1 D 24    BARBARA: Why should we?
4-s DOCTOR/SUSAN/    What reason could we have?
BARBARA/IAN

98. 2 D 16    DOCTOR: Blackmail! You
MS BARBARA    wanted to force me to return
you to England.

BARBARA: Don't be ridiculous!

99. 1 D 24    DOCTOR: I'm sure of it!
2-s DOCTOR & BARB.    BARBARA: How dare you! Do
you realise, you stupid old
man, that you'd have died in
the Cave of Skulls if Ian
hadn't made fire for you?
And what about the terrible
things we went through against
100. 2 D 16    the Daleks? You tricked us
2-s BARBARA & DOC.    into going down into the
City. Accuse us? You ought
to go down on your knees and
101. 1 D 24    thank us. But gratitude is
3-s BARBARA/SUSAN/DOC.    the last thing you'll ever
have. Or any sort of
commonsense, either!

(2 next)

---

(Cam. 1 on sh.101)    (SHE WALKS AWAY TO
THE CLOCK IN A FURY)

CRANE L., LOSE
BARBARA, PICK    SUSAN: She's talking sense,
UP IAN R/O/F.    Grandfather.

(THE DOCTOR DOES NOT
REPLY.

102. 2 D 33    BARBARA SCREAMS.
LOW CLOSE S. BARBARA.    IAN GOES TO HER)

103. 3 F 9    IAN: Barbara!
CU CLOCK FACE    (SHOW CLOCK FACE IN
C.U.
ALL THE NUMBERS HAVE
MELTED CONSIDERABLY.
ALTHOUGH THE ORIGINAL
FIGURES ARE CLEAR
ENOUGH, THEY ARE
MISSHAPEN AND
104. 2 D 33    FRIGHTENING.
TIGHT 3-s BARBARA/    IAN LOOKS AT HIS
IAN/SUSAN.    OWN WRISTWATCH.

105. 4 G    C.U. IAN'S WRISTWATCH.
CU WRISTWATCH

106. 2 D 33    THE SAME THING HAS
3-s BARBARA/IAN/SUSAN    HAPPENED.

107. 1 D 16    BARBARA GLANCES AT
3-s SUSAN/BARBARA/IAN    HERS, TOO.
BARBARA TAKES OFF HER
WATCH AND THROWS IT AT
THE CONTROL PANEL.
THERE IS A FLASH.

DOCTOR RUBS HIS CHIN
THOUGHTFULLY, THEN
HE WALKS AWAY -
SLIGHT PAUSE - )

SUSAN: We're somewhere where
time doesn't exist; where
nothing exists except us.

(3 next)

---

(Cam. 1 on sh. 107)

108. 3 F 24    LS DOCTOR

109. 1 D 33    4-s.

110.

can
cor.

WITH
FOUR

AND
RBARA)

ded we need
're somewhat
Chesterton....
usan...
CUPS)

nderstood you,
nute you abuse
you play the

ttle nightcap
l relax and sleep.

HIS)

is night. We've no
ing, have we?

JOINS IAN AND
OCTOR)

I'm going to bed.

Make it up with her,
ather, please do.

OCTOR LOOKS AT BARBARA,
HO IS SLIGHTLY AWAY
ROM THE GROUP. SHE
BECOMES AWARE THE
DOCTOR IS LOOKING AT HER,
MOVES AND GOES INTO THE
LIVING QUARTERS.
SUSAN FOLLOWS WITH A
REPROACHFUL LOOK AT
THE DOCTOR)

30 -

(Cam. 2 on sh. 110) - 31 -

IAN: Doctor, very strange things are happening. I think we're in very great danger. This is no time for personal quarrels.

DOCTOR: Meaning?

IAN: I think you should go and apologise to Barbara.

111. 3 24
TIGHT 2-s

DOCTOR: Young man. I am not concerned with codes of manners when poised in the cosmos. I don't underestimate our danger any more than you do. But I must have time to think.

PULL BACK WITH THEM

(THEY START TO MOVE TOWARD THE LIVING QUARTERS)

DOCTOR: A rash action is worse than no action at all.

IAN: I don't see anything rash in apologising to Barbara.

112. 1 B 24

/BOOM B3

CAMS:1B,4C,4E,2D,1E,3.

10. INT. THE LIVING QUARTERS. SHIP.

IAN: I find it very hard to keep pace with you.

DOCTOR: Don't you mean one jump ahead? And that you never will be. You need my knowledge and then the ability to apply it - and then you need my experience to gain the fullest results.

IAN: Results for good? Or for evil?

(4 next)

(Cam. 1 on sh. 112) - 32 -

DOCTOR: One man's law may be another man's crime. Sleep on that, Chesterton. Sleep on it.

TRACK IN TO C.U. IAN.

(DOCTOR.MOVES OUT OF SHOT.
C.U. IAN'S FACE.)

113. 4 C 33
WIDE 2-s

/BOOM #1/

11. INT. BARBARA'S BED.

(BARBARA IS WEARING AN ATTRACTIVE NIGHTROBE.
SUSAN COMES INTO SHOT)

SUSAN: I just came to say I'm sorry for what Grandfather said.

BARBARA: It wasn't your fault.

SUSAN: I know. But...try and understand him. Forgive him.

PUSH IN TO C.U. BARBARA.

(BARBARA SMILES AT SUSAN)

BARBARA: Try and get some sleep.

(SUSAN NODS AND GOES OUT OF SHOT. BARBARA SITS ON HER BED. SUDDENLY SHE LOOKS ABOUT HER. SHE IS CONSCIOUS OF BEING ALONE.

FADE./

114. 4 E 24
BARBARA F/G.
DOCTOR COMES TO HER.
LET HIM GO OUT OF SHOT.

FADE UP.
BARBARA IS NOW ASLEEP.
IT IS SOME TIME LATER.
(contd...)

(1 next)

- 32 -

the strange events continue, open hostility breaks out. The Doctor accuses the two schoolteachers of sabotaging the ship as a blackmail threat to get them back to England in their own time. Susan goes temporarily berserk and viciously wields a pair of scissors at Ian. And Barbara, fed up with the Doctor's taunts, gives him a piece of her mind, telling him he should be grateful for all their help.

The crisis point comes when the Doctor, unable to fathom what has happened, decides to put the two teachers off the ship.

Suddenly the whole of the Fault Locator lights up, showing that all the controls of the TARDIS have broken down. The Doctor realises that there is no way the two teachers could have achieved all this, but it is Barbara who arrives at the real solution.

It is the TARDIS itself which has halted their flight, aware of some danger which the time-travellers themselves are not. Reviewing the procedures he followed on leaving Skaro, the Doctor, at last, traces the fault – a tiny broken spring on a switch that, had it stayed in the 'down' position, would have sent the TARDIS back past the moment when the Earth's solar system was formed – beyond the Sun's point of creation. The ship refused to do this, knowing it would be destroyed, and immobilised itself, using what techniques it could to warn the travellers. With the spring repaired the systems come back on again, and the Doctor is able to reset the controls for Earth.

Tempers cool but the Doctor realises that he said some terrible things to his unwilling passengers. Barbara in particular is less than sympathetic towards him, but the old man eventually pours oil on troubled waters by explaining that as they travel together, so they will learn more of each other.

The TARDIS lands on a snowy plateau. The readings say Earth, but outside Susan finds the footprint of a giant in the snow.

**Background:** This remarkable two-part adventure came about purely as a stop-gap measure to forestall a looming crisis.

Work preparing the 'Marco Polo' story for the studio had taken up more time and resources than was originally envisaged. Designed to be a showpiece for the new series, the very ambitious script, even in its final form, called for every stage in Polo's journey to Peking from the Himalayas to be represented with sumptuous interior sets, exterior sets done in the studio, animated map graphics, and a vast array of costumes, props and backdrops.

It was a mammoth undertaking and, as work on 'The Daleks' story began to wind down, the awful truth dawned that 'Marco Polo' would not be ready in time to make its booked studio allocation.

The knock-on effect of this would be to delay the start of *Doctor Who* on Television, something considered very unwise in the light of problems encountered on 'The Daleks'.

The compromise was a filler story which would make good use of the available studio. The only problem was that only the regular cast could be used and the only set could be the TARDIS.

Working against time, David Whitaker is believed to have put together the first of his two fifty page scripts in one afternoon – taking the opportunity to introduce viewers further to the characters of the Doctor, Ian, Barbara and Susan, and to make more known about the TARDIS space/time ship.

Problems did not cease either with production of the second script. Engaging a Director proved far from easy as Verity Lambert discovered. Having to rely on staff Directors in-between other assignments, she found her first choice, Paddy Russell, unavailable at the last moment, and second choice, Richard Martin, only free for one episode. Finally Frank Cox was pulled in to shoot part two.

The cast also found the story difficult to rehearse, experiencing problems interpreting many of Whitaker's ideas on concussed behaviour.

Ironically, the only person with a fairly easy passage on this show was Raymond Cusick. Peter Brachaki's TARDIS control room set made up the bulk of the design requirements, leaving Cusick only with the task of constructing two dormitory rooms.

Stock, copyright-cleared, library music overcame the show's lack of budget and time for the commissioning of specially composed incidental music.

Originally without a generic title, this serial has eventually become known by four names: 'The Spaceship', 'Inside The Spaceship', 'Beyond The Sun' (a hangover from the retitling of Malcolm Hulke's story 'The Hidden Planet') and 'The Edge of Destruction'.

## Production Credits

Serial 'C'
Two Episodes
Black and White

'The Edge Of
Destruction'
'The Brink Of Disaster'

8 February 1964
15 February 1964

### Cast
Doctor Who          William Hartnell
Ian Chesterton      William Russell
Barbara Wright      Jacqueline Hill
Susan Foreman       Carole Ann Ford

### Crew
Production Assistant       Tony Lightley
Assistant Floor Manager    Jeremy Hare
Costume Supervisor         Daphne Dare
Make-up Supervisor         Ann Ferriggi
Story Editor               David Whitaker
Designer                   Raymond Cusick
Associate Producer         Mervyn Pinfield
Director (1)               Richard Martin
Director (2)               Frank Cox

# THE MYTH MAKERS

DAVID WHITAKER'S appointment, picking up the gauntlet of Newman's challenge to make *Doctor Who* a science fiction Theatre-of-the-Air, was not quite a moment instantly recognisable as a turning point in Television history. In fact, with any number of other writers, the circumstances of the appointment could well have been self-appraised as, 'Oh no, not more work.'

As his first wife, June Barry, recalls, Whitaker was at work on another project when a knock at the office door heralded the entrance of Donald Wilson. With an air of urgency, suggesting that he had a host of other people to see, Wilson handed over a four-page programme guide with a curt: 'It's called *Doctor Who*. It's science fiction set in a London police box. I'd like you to write it up for me. Away you go.' Then, having deposited the folder of foolscap pages on Whitaker's desk, the Head of Serials made as rapid a departure as he had made an entrance.

Allowing for the vagaries of memory, plus some very likely embellishing in the way Whitaker recounted the tale to his, then, fiancée, it is possible that the above tale contains just a couple of overt simplifications. Nevertheless, even catering for the eloquence of the after-dinner story teller, this abrupt introduction of *Doctor Who* into the Serials Department does serve to give an insight into two men who shaped much of what later went before the cold eyes of the BBC cameras.

Donald Wilson was very much of the BBC's 'old school' which had grown up in the wake of Lord Reith. It was Reith who had imbued the BBC with the mystique of a divine right to broadcast – laying down so many of the standards which raised the values of the Corporation to a par with any Civil Service division.

A great student of literature and the classics, Donald Wilson, described by many who knew him as an 'avuncular Scot with an enormous sense of humour', had been more than capable of helming the BBC's Drama Unit up to its dissolution by Sydney Newman. He was a firm believer in the power of Television, seeing it as a definitive medium for enriching the lives of the general public through the art of its broadcasting.

Divid Whitaker, the first script-editor of *Doctor Who*, and the man responsible for creating much of the magic of the programme.

This was the appeal of *Doctor Who* in his eyes. Its wide-ranging format allowed children's costume drama, previously thought the sole preserve of the Classic Serials Division, to be made more appealing by means of a link to the space age. An even greater attraction was the additional dramatic layer of having the Doctor and his friends as hindsight judge and jury over the events surrounding them. Their presence, either in medieval England or aboard a space rocket, situated them ideally as narrators; to offer explanations of everything from the Battle of Hastings to nuclear propulsion.

*Doctor Who*, though, was not going to be a straight children's serial, since its main aim in life was to capture the family audience between *Grandstand* and *Juke Box Jury*. Partly in recompense for disbanding Wilson's Drama Department, Newman gave the assignment to him with the expressed intention of fostering a year-round drama serial suitable for all age groups: the drive for class – indivisible Television to cross all boundaries and backgrounds. It is doubtful that the Children's Department could have made the series anyway, as one of Sydney Newman's other shake-ups had been to wind down this Department, dispersing much of its talent throughout the rest of the Drama Group.

So *Doctor Who* could not be obvious in its audience approach. Unlike generations of 'So tell me, Professor . . .' presentations, geared at younger audiences, the show's appeal would be upwards of *Whirligig*, but pitched to fall short of the gut horror depicted in the *Quatermass* dramas or Robert Gould's 1962 serial *The Big Pull*, which had centred around the biological perils of sending astronauts through the Earth's radiation belt.

Like any good manager Donald Wilson chose David Whitaker to story edit *Doctor Who* because he felt he was the best man for the job. But how had he arrived at this conclusion?

David Whitaker was born in Knebworth, Hertfordshire in 1928, although fairly soon afterwards his family moved to Barnes in South-West London where he went to school and spent much of his adolescent life.

Two great, but quite contrasting, literary loves manifested themselves early on, both of which were to have an influence on his later *Doctor Who* career. On the one hand Whitaker was a keen devotee of science fiction, with Ray Bradbury in particular a favourite. On the other hand, Whitaker avidly devoured the kind of *Boy's Own* adventures typified by such heroes as Bulldog Drummond and any of John Buchan's creations.

Theatre became his first professional ground-base: writing for, appearing in and directing productions for a wide number of companies, including the celebrated York Repertory Group. It was while he was with York Rep that one of his plays, *A Choice of Partners* was seen in production by a member of the BBC Script Unit. The BBC subsequently bought the broadcasting rights to the play and commissioned David Whitaker to adapt it for Television. On its merits Donald Wilson asked, in 1957, if Whitaker would do a three month trial as an in-house writer.

For the next few years, David Whitaker immersed himself in all aspects of writing for Television. He wrote six plays, contributed episodes to many series and serials (both as a writer and a Story Editor), all of which went into production, including a successful series about a pilot-adventurer called *Garry Halliday*: a mixture somewhere between *Biggles* and *Bulldog Drummond*. He also provided lyrics for a musical (Whitaker was an accomplished pianist) and even wrote comedy links for several variety shows.

As a person, Whitaker was frequently described by those who knew him as a great store-house of energy and enthusiasm, who could manage that rare gift of imparting such enthusiasm to others. On the surface, he was a very outgoing man, frequently in the company of esteemed names from the showbusiness profession. James Beck (late of *Dad's Army*) was among his closest friends, while on the romantic side he almost got engaged to Yootha Joyce, got engaged to Justine Lord, and then finally, in the summer of 1963, mid-way through his work setting up *Doctor Who*, got married to June Barry, soon to gain world-wide fame herself as one of the three leading ladies in Donald Wilson's epic adaption of John Galsworthy's *The Forsyte Saga*.

What made Whitaker ideal for *Doctor Who*, though, was his ability to write from the heart; to put into words notions and understandings of wonder. June Barry explains:

'David was a tremendous lateral thinker. He'd look at a problem and come up with a totally different answer to the one you'd expect . . . As a person, David was almost a man born out of his period. He had impeccable manners that somehow always reminded you of an older, bygone age. He never lost his links with children either. He could always talk to them on their level without ever sounding patronising, as most adults tend to do.'

Whatever specific qualities Donald Wilson observed in Whitaker's style of writing, and saw as suitable for *Doctor Who*, can only be guessed at, but it is very likely he saw in Whitaker the sought-after bridge of writing for adults and writing for children. He could link both with a talent for seeing the future and the past from a sideways, yet very humanly understandable, perspective – in short, bringing out the magic of travelling in the fourth dimension to the audience sitting at home.

Intrigued by Sydney Newman's two-page memo Donald Wilson first took it to BBC staff writer C. E. 'Bunny' Webber, whose job it became to flesh out the synopsis into something suitable for a Script-Editor to work from. Webber's job was to locate any pitfalls in the concept which might give substance to Wilson's original 'maybe' about the show. Then, if any of them looked like causing serious narrative or production headaches Webber, in consultation with Wilson and Newman, could make appropriate adjustments before writers were commissioned. Webber is believed to have refined the four characters, devised by Newman, into the essential dipolar structure by which most long-running serials operate, namely conflict. The Doctor and his teenage companion would be the doyens of one alien culture, whose morality and attitudes would lead them into opposition with the two human characters.

60

Other rules, too, needed to be followed. The two sets of characters needed to be able to confide in one another. Only by such means could motivations be established and explained without resort to one of Television's phoniest cop-outs – the character who consistently talks to himself, to the point of ultimately causing the audience to have serious doubts about that character's sanity.

There were sound technical reasons for keeping the regular cast no smaller than four. The medium of continuous recording prompted the inclusion of bridging scenes to allow one group of characters time to go off one set and onto another while the action is carried on by the second group of characters. Reasoning that the very nature of *Doctor Who* would mean scenes at the beginning and end of serials where only the regular cast were involved, this element became almost a prerequisite to production.

Under Webber's experienced eye Sydney Newman's memo became a four page document. It was this which Donald Wilson studied, approved, and finally placed before David Whitaker, whose job it would now be to develop ideas into stories.

Whitaker read Sydney Newman's brief and was immediately captivated by its premise to link the fantastic with the ordinary. Everyone expects, he reasoned, to see large, gleaming spaceships orbiting planets. But what if the spaceships were here already, disguised as everyday artifacts? And what if their occupants were already walking among us, keeping cautiously in the background to avoid notice and suspicion, just as twentieth-century man would need to do if he were thrust into another, and potentially hostile, age.

It was important, Whitaker felt, to keep alive the awe and slight fear felt by strangers in strange lands – whether they be aliens in the twentieth century, or 1963 members of the general public in twelfth-century Cathay.

He drew up a very elaborate Writer's Guide to explain what he had in mind to the authors he planned to canvass for *Doctor Who*. Quality was Whitaker's prime consideration in realising Newman's brief. Whatever else happened, in what could be a very technically limiting production, *Doctor Who* would be founded by the best writers he could afford. And that meant taking a trip down to the lower end of the Bayswater Road.

Some years earlier, Ray Galton and Alan Simpson (the writers for comic artist Tony Hancock) and Goon comedian Spike Milligan had established Associated London Scripts (A.L.S.), an institution described by June Barry as 'a hot bed of writers, many of whom had offices in the house which they rented out to use whenever they wanted to get away from home or from the studios.'

A.L.S. afforded Whitaker a groundswell of proven Television writers, many with a wide experience of writing science fiction. It is interesting to note that of the fourteen scripts Whitaker eventually commissioned for *Doctor Who*, no less than nine of them hailed from the pens of A.L.S. writers, with himself writing a further three.

Interesting too is the web of connections with *Doctor Who*'s 'Godfather'. Dennis Spooner, John Lucarotti and Bill Strutton were veterans of *The Avengers*, a Sydney Newman creation. Malcolm Hulke was a creater of *Pathfinders*, while Terry Nation, a close friend of Dennis Spooner, had contributed a sf script to ABC TV for a series called *Out of this World*, script-edited by Irene Shubik, soon to be brought to the BBC herself by Sydney Newman to helm his adult science fiction anthology series *Out of the Unknown*, destined for the new channel, BBC 2.

One name conspicuous by its absence was that of Nigel Kneale, whom Whitaker contacted very early on. Kneale read the synopsis but felt the format too whimsical to fit his much grimmer style of writing. Teaching history or science to children was, he felt, just not his style.

Right from the very start Whitaker defined the structure of *Doctor Who* as alternating stories between past and future. A historical adventure would be followed by a science fiction tale, then by another historical, and so on.

Interpreting Sydney Newman and Donald Wilson's ideas literally, Whitaker asked each of his 'historical' authors to include sequences with famous figures of the past: Nero, Napoleon, Marco Polo and so on. Of the science fiction writers he asked that each serial should explore and extrapolate on a known scientific or cultural theme, such as nuclear war, doppler imaging or xenophobia. Even the quest for fire, an element of nature taken for granted in the twentieth century, Whitaker felt could be held up as an artifact of wonder through the medium of *Doctor Who*.

For this reason David Whitaker chose the harnassing of fire by Neanderthal man as the subject for the first adventure. It seemed to blend best Newman's two dictates for the show. The abrupt transition from 1963 London to the Paleolithic era would emphasise the Doctor's time-travelling capabilities, while the sub-plot of making fire, crucial to the narrative, would bring home to the audience the key to the human race's survival made by its 'discovery'.

As the Spring of 1963 gave way to Summer, one priority became uppermost in Whitaker's mind – to get one script of each type of *Doctor Who* story together as soon as possible. This would have two benefits. Firstly it would demonstrate to prospective freelance writers the type of material required. Secondly, and most important, it would lay the foundation stones of the series from which the myth could be built. Placing great importance on this latter aspect Whitaker decided the first two scripts should be written by the same author, who would thus maintain an overall series continuity. For this reason, and realising it would need to be a writer based at the BBC with whom he could work closely, David Whitaker, on Donald Wilson's recommendation, selected Anthony Coburn.

Anthony Coburn got the commission to write the first story by a notable stroke of good fortune. Some years beforehand the Writer's Guild of Great Britain (a kind of trade union for authors) had been in correspondance with its opposite number in Australia. Concerned by their distinct lack of success in 'culturally acceptable mass media writing', the Australians had turned to Britain for tutoring. Eventually an agreement was fixed whereby budding Australian authors could come to Britain and learn from their peers the art and craft of writing for stage, screen and Television. In return, it was promised, British writers would find no problems getting work permits 'down under'.

Throughout the Sixties many Australian writers made the pilgrimage to England, with Anthony Coburn and Bill Strutton being just two of them who landed on the steps of A.L.S.

Whitaker, a committed and active Guild member, recognised in Coburn a considerable talent and so offered him the not insubstantial opportunity to shape a BBC drama series from grass roots, by writing its pilot.

Coburn wrote his first four part storyline in two sections, starting with the quest for fire plot, which he named 'The Tribe of Gum' before going back to the very first episode, which had to be a more collaborative effort with the Script-Editor and the Producers. At the time of Coburn's first draft little was settled either on the casting front or on the design aspects of the Doctor's space/time machine – key factors as they were greatly dependent on the size of the budget which would be allocated the show.

Ultimately, a figure of £2,500 per episode was fixed by the planners, a result which had as much effect on the script side as it did on the production values.

In his guidelines, Sydney Newman had recommended between four and six episodes as ideal for each *Doctor Who* serial. Any longer than an absolute maximum of six, he argued, would run the risk of not being able to recapture viewers lost to an unpopular first episode.

Following this brief, Whitaker had gone ahead commissioning a crop of four part stories to make up the twelve shows needed to keep *Doctor Who* on air for forty-eight weeks – one year in BBC terms, allowing for Christmas, sports events and other potential breaks.

The stated budget, however, meant some drastic rethinking. Estimates to design all the elaborate sets, costumes and props for the science fiction shows were coming in, and they were not cheap. Even the historical travelogues, with their resource to tap existing stocks of costumes and sets, were not proving that great as money savers. Something had to go.

Eventual casualties were principles and scripts. Desirable though the four parters might be story-wise, both Whitaker and Verity Lambert recognised the expense overheads in having so many 'first nights' (ie: new serials with new props, sets, cast, etc.). In monetary terms it made a lot more sense to extend episode numbers within a serial, thereby getting more television hours with fewer changes in location.

The full quota of how many and whose scripts went west in this rethink will probably never be known. The only title officially identified as having been lost was Malcolm Hulke's teleplay, 'The

OVERLEAF:
The first crewmembers of the TARDIS: the Doctor (William Hartnell) and Susan (Carole Ann Ford) and their two human companions Ian (William Russell) and Barbara (Jacqueline Hill).

Hidden Planet', which explored the idea of Earth having an identical twin diametrically opposite on the far side of the Sun. For *Doctor Who* this was a sad loss. Not only was it a loss to the series of Malcolm Hulke for a good many years, it was also a nail in the coffin of the show's bid to be genuinely educative.

Several of the remaining stories needed the grafting of an extra episode – a move ultimately contributary towards the whole shift in emphasis *Doctor Who* underwent before it even reached the TV screens.

Coburn's first story, however, was kept inviolate. It had to be, if only succinctly to show the BBC and, later, the audience at home, what the series was all about.

David Whitaker devised the balance of the four main characters, drawing, perhaps predictably, from the literature close to his heart. Hero of the series would be Ian Chesterton, an everyday individual catapulted, like Richard Hannay in *The Thirty Nine Steps*, from suburban normality into a fight for survival, armed only with wits, ingenuity and physical prowess. Like Hannay, Chesterton would adapt quickly to the strangeness of his new environment, evolving into a pillar of strength on whom the audience knew they could depend in times of crisis.

In Whitaker's character brief to writers, Ian was stipulated as being a teacher of applied science, a 27-year-old graduate from an English 'red brick' university on whom the Doctor's teenage companion might have a crush. He would be a good physical specimen, a gymnast, dexterous with his hands and patient enough to deal with the Doctor in his irascible moods. He would occasionally clash with the Doctor on decisions, but would be able to make intelligent enquiry and bring sound common sense to bear in moments of stress.

Perhaps not a million miles from Hannay's unwilling female companion in *The Thirty Nine Steps* was Barbara Wright, the human element in the series. Whereas Ian would be resourceful and brave, Barbara would be the voice of reason, relating their experiences in human terms. She would stoically accept her role as a prisoner in space, coming to terms with it as Whitaker believed any balanced individual would do.

Whitaker's notes refer to Barbara as 'an attractive 23-year-old history teacher, timid, but capable of sudden courage'. There was no initial prospect of romance between her and Ian, but it was suggested her admiration for the man would sometimes lead to under-currents of antagonism between her and Susan.

In formulating the Doctor, Whitaker drew on literature's most famous detective, Sherlock Holmes. Conan Doyle's celebrated creation had never been fully explained in the books, the ploy of writing the novels from Doctor Watson's perspective avoiding any need to explain or qualify Holmes's astonishing brilliance and motivation.

This, in similar vein, was what David Whitaker wanted for the Doctor. Newman's guidelines had advised 'old, crotchety, senile but brilliant' for the personality. Whitaker added, and stressed, the qualities of enigma, mystery and remoteness. People would marvel at his cleverness, but they would never understand the person beneath it. In Whitaker's eyes the suffix *Who* in the Doctor's title would refer to mystery rather than amnesia.

The fourth member of the party, Newman had said, should be a teenage girl from the Doctor's home planet – a modern figure identifiable to the younger age-group *Doctor Who* was hoping to attract. This role was initially left somewhat vague until Anthony Coburn advanced the suggestion she should be the Doctor's granddaughter. Whitaker considered this notion and approved its inclusion in the script.

Between them, Whitaker and Coburn devised the first episode's opening in an English school. Susan had persuaded her grandfather to let her spend some time in this era to gain an appreciation of its customs and opportunities. However, being an alien, her astonishing depths of knowledge in some spheres, coupled with incredible ignorance in others, would be the trigger to launch Ian and Barbara on their quest to discover the truth about her.

Reportedly Coburn also advanced the name TARDIS to represent the bridge between how the ship would appear on the outside, and its size inside, namely Time And Relative Dimensions In Space – a neat piece of apocrypha to side-step explaining the revolutionary media sf concept of not having the space-ship's interior at all resemble its exterior.

Having fleshed out the frames of the characters, Whitaker virtually gave Coburn a free hand in his teleplay, needing to concentrate instead on the vast amount of work involved in reshaping the series with the loss or deferment of so many storylines.

Foremost among his worries was a storyline from a writer initially recommended to him by Dennis Spooner – Terry Nation. After first of all declining to write for the series, Nation eventually agreed after a row with his former employer, comedian Tony Hancock, left him with no income to pay for a central heating system he was having installed at home.

But, as things transpired, it was Nation's eventual storyline, initially titled 'The Mutants' that was to set the seal on the way the science fiction stories would be handled within *Doctor Who*'s structure.

Although happy at first with the series concept as handed to him by Donald Wilson, David Whitaker's under-lying love for 'ripping yarn' storytelling was threatening to draw him into conflict with Newman's wish to present educative and allegorical discussion of social issues within the show's framework. Matters came to a head when Anthony Coburn delivered his second storyline, a science fiction adventure set on thirtieth-century Earth, titled simply 'The Robots'.

At this time in the planet's history the human race had become extinct, having perished by some global catastrophe, and had been succeeded by their immortal robot servants. These highly intelligent androids, perfect except for their total inability to think creatively, had devised a super robot which they intended should lead them. However, no sooner had they built such a machine than they recognised in it the inherent dangers of a heartless device capable of original thought. Accepting the only logical course of action the robots had shut down the machine, even though it meant they too sank into inertia as a consequence.

Into this situation would arrive the time-travellers who, not knowing the reason behind the world's stagnation, would re-activate first the robots and then the machine, learning to their cost that heartless, electronic megalomania is infinitely worse than emotion-based megalomania.

The standpoint of Coburn's story was an extrapolation of machine intelligence, written at a time when computers were only just beginning to encroach into the commercial environment of Britain.

It was an intelligent, thought-provoking script, but in Whitaker's eyes it just did not work. The vital ingredient of popular appeal was not there despite several bids to rejig the story. Comparing it with Nation's material produced a no-contest winner.

The aftermath of Whitaker junking 'The Robots' in favour of 'The Mutants' as the sf showpiece story will probably never be known, particularly as both writers are now dead. What is noticeable, however, is that Anthony Coburn never wrote for the series again after 'The Tribe of Gum', and even on that story he did none of the rewriting which followed the less-than-successful screening of the pilot episode to BBC Department heads.

However, while 'The Robots' did little to galvanise Whitaker's enthusiasm, Terry Nation's story certainly did. It was only the third script to be completed (Coburn's 'The Tribe of Gum' serial, retitled 'Doctor Who and 100,000 BC', and John Lucarotti's 'Journey to Cathay' preceding it), but at once Whitaker felt he had found the right niche for *Doctor Who*'s presentation of science fiction. 'The Mutants' later to be renamed 'The Daleks', was a morality play, but with the moral element very much left of the centre stage which belonged, quite rightly he felt, to a straightforward clash between good and evil.

What attracted Whitaker greatly to 'The Daleks' was the mythology aspect of the story. Throughout the script were continual references to the history of Skaro, the background of the Thals, the evolution of the Daleks and the strangeness of their world. Like the Greek and Egyptian legends of old, here was material to fire the imagination of writer, reader and viewer alike – broad in its scope and with a fine attention to detail. Terry Nation had succeeded in carving a foreign world every bit as believable as Lucarotti's carefully researched account of life in twelfth-century Cathay.

When, later, 'The Daleks' took the viewing public by storm David Whitaker contributed every bit as much as Terry Nation to the wave of Dalekmania which threatened to overwhelm the toyshops, book counters, newspaper stands, cinema aisles and theatre seats of Great Britain.

His passionate belief in the strength of the *Doctor Who* ethos saw

The Dalek comic strip from *TV21* which David Whitaker scripted between 1965 and 1966. The strip concluded with the Daleks discovering Earth's location, thereby acting as a prequel for the TV story 'The Dalek Invasion of Earth'.

# THE DALEKS

The Daleks search for the last of their original race—unaware they are near to discovering a new solar system . . . which contains the planet Earth...

BELOW, IN THE MOUNTAIN CHAMBER...

MAGNIFICENT! AND ONLY YOU AND I KNOW OF THIS DISTANT PLANET, LODIAN?

YES, THAT IS EARTH, ZET, TEEMING WITH LIFE, RICH IN MINERAL WEALTH, ALWAYS LEARNING AND IMPROVING.

THINK WHAT THOSE METAL MONSTERS WOULD DO TO EARTH.

AND THINK WHAT THE DALEKS WOULD GIVE TO KNOW THIS SECRET!

THEY WILL GIVE ME POWER! MAKE ME THEIR LEADER... I, ZET, WILL BE RULER OF THE SKY.

MEANWHILE, THE METAL DALEKS HAVE FOUND A WAY INTO THE MOUNTAIN...

THE PASSAGE SHOWS SIGNS OF INTELLIGENT LIFE, BUT THE SNOW STORM PREVENTS OUR TRANSMITTING SCANNER RELAYING THESE PICTURES...

CENTRAL CONTROL, WE HAVE FOUND A LARGE FACTORY INSIDE THE MOUNTAIN. AS YET, NO EVIDENCE OF LIFE.

THE DALEKS REACH THE FIRST CHAMBER...

I AM ZET. TAKE ME TO YOUR LEADER AND I PROMISE YOU THE CONQUEST OF THE SKIES!

BUT AS THE DALEKS CARRY HIM AWAY, LODIAN REGAINS CONSCIOUSNESS...

SOMEHOW... I'VE GOT TO STOP THEM DISCOVERING EARTH!

WE WILL TAKE YOU TO OUR CITY. IS THE OTHER LIFE-FORM DEAD? IF SO, LEAVE HIM.

NO, LODIAN IS THE KEY TO THE SUPREMACY OF THE DALEKS.

him extending its repertoire into a whole range of media. He wrote two novels for Frederick Muller Ltd based on the series, and the very first *Doctor Who* annual for World Distributors. He co-authored the first Dalek movie, and wrote dialogue for the second virtually single-handedly. He penned the 1964 stage play, *Curse of the Daleks*, and spent two years writing all the back page Dalek comic strips for *TV 21*, only to see much of the credit for all the above going – with the royalties – to Terry Nation. As a BBC employee, Whitaker could only receive his monthly salary. Anything he pioneered, created or evolved for the series, up to his resignation from the BBC in 1964, was owned lock, stock and barrel by the Corporation.

Despite living virtually in the shadow of Terry Nation all through his *Doctor Who* career, Whitaker was the natural choice when Gerry Davis and Sydney Newman came to revise the Doctor's character for Patrick Troughton in 1966. Newman especially had faith in Whitaker as the ideal weaver of *Doctor Who* stories. As June Barry sums up:

'David crafted and shaped *Doctor Who*. Sydney and Donald evolved the frame, but the myth came from him.

'He worked harder on the show than anyone else, steering many of the writers he brought into *Doctor Who*. And he created far more than he is ever given credit for . . .'

70

# THE KEYS OF MARINUS

The Cusick Stories
Serial 'E'

**Synopsis:** The many continents of the planet Marinus are the settings for this six part adventure as the Doctor's party find themselves on a quest to locate the missing keys to the Conscience of Marinus.

The TARDIS lands on the shores of an island surrounded by a sea of acid. At the island's summit is the magnificent pyramid which houses the Conscience Machine – a massive artifact built centuries ago to bring peace to this once-troubled world. The machine works by erasing emotions from the minds of the peoples of Marinus, substituting tranquillity and calm for aggression and greed. Recently, however, its power has been waning.

The black masked Voord, led by the power-hungry Yartek, have taken advantage of the machine's weakening energies to develop an Immuniser. Now they are intent upon capturing the Conscience to use its influence for their own ends.

All this the Doctor and his group learn from the aged Keeper of the Conscience, Arbitan. He further explains that before the machine can be operated five micro-circuit keys must be in place.

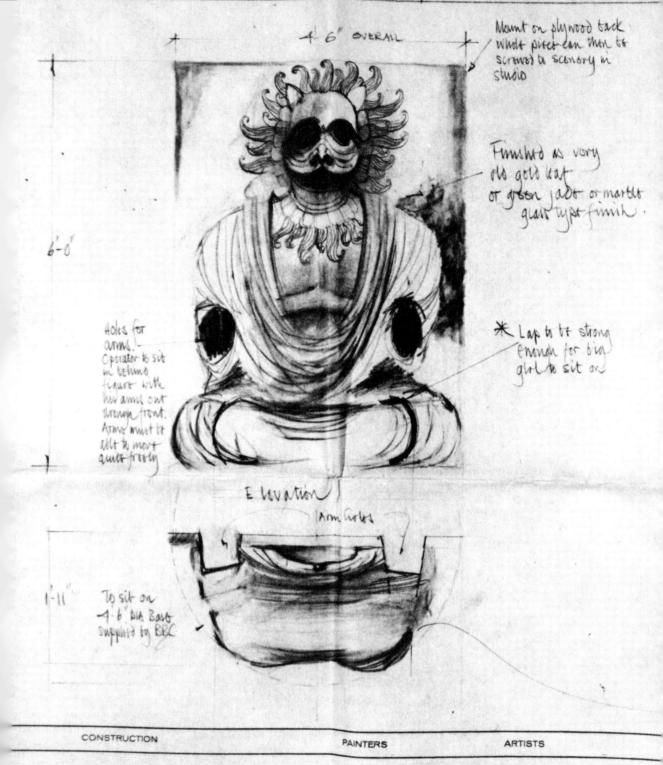

↑ 6" OVERALL

Mount on plywood back whole piece can then be screwed to scenery in studio

Finished as very old gold leaf or green jade or marble glass type finish.

6'-0"

Holes for arms. Operator to sit in behind figure with his arms out through front. Arms must be able to move quite freely

* Lap to be strong enough for big girl to sit on

Elevation

Arm Holes

1'-11"

To sit on 4'-6" Dia Base supplied by BBC

| CONSTRUCTION | PAINTERS | ARTISTS |
| --- | --- | --- |

* AS ABOVE   X   BY DISCUSSION   WITH   DESIGNE

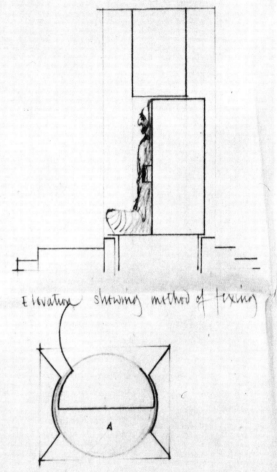

Elevation showing method of fixing

A

OUTSIDE CONTRACTOR: DESIGN & DISPLAY LTD.

STOCK

**BBC tv** DESIGN DEPARTMENT

| | |
|---|---|
| SHEET NO. 1 | DATE DRAWN 24/3/64 |
| NO. OF SHEETS 1 | SCALE 1½" |

DISTRIBUTION

| | | | | |
|---|---|---|---|---|
| ☐ ALLOCATIONS | ☐ DESIGNER EALING | ☑ PRODUCER | |
| ☐ A.P.M. (TEL) | ☐ DESIGN ORGANISER 2 | ☑ SCENE MASTER | |
| ☐ BACK PROJECTION | ☐ DRAPES | ☑ ASST. SCENEMASTER | |
| ☐ GRAPHICS | ☑ ELECTRICIANS | ☑ SCENERY STORES | |
| ☐ CARPENTERS | ☑ ESTIMATOR | ☐ SCENIC ARTISTS | |
| ☐ CON. MANAGER | ☐ F.M's OFFICE | ☑ SPECIAL EFFECTS | |
| ☑ DESIGNER | ☐ METAL WORKERS | ☑ SUPPLY FOREMAN | |
| ☐ DESIGN ASST. | ☐ PAINTERS | ☐ SUPPLY ORGANISER | |
| ☑ PROPS | ☑ VERITY LAMBERT | ☑ OUTSIDE CONTRACTOR | |

| | |
|---|---|
| ESTIMATOR | PRODUCER JOHN GORRIE |
| *(signature)* | DESIGNER RAYMOND P. CUSICK Nº 2435 |
| | DRAWN BY |
| DATE 24 3 64 | ZERO DATE 25/3/64  V.T.R. DATE |
| | FILM DATE    TRANS DATE 27/3/64 |
| *(signature)* | PRODUCTION |
| DATE | DR WHO Nº 3 SERIES B |
| STUDIO D  4/64 | PRODUCTION NUMBER 2398 |

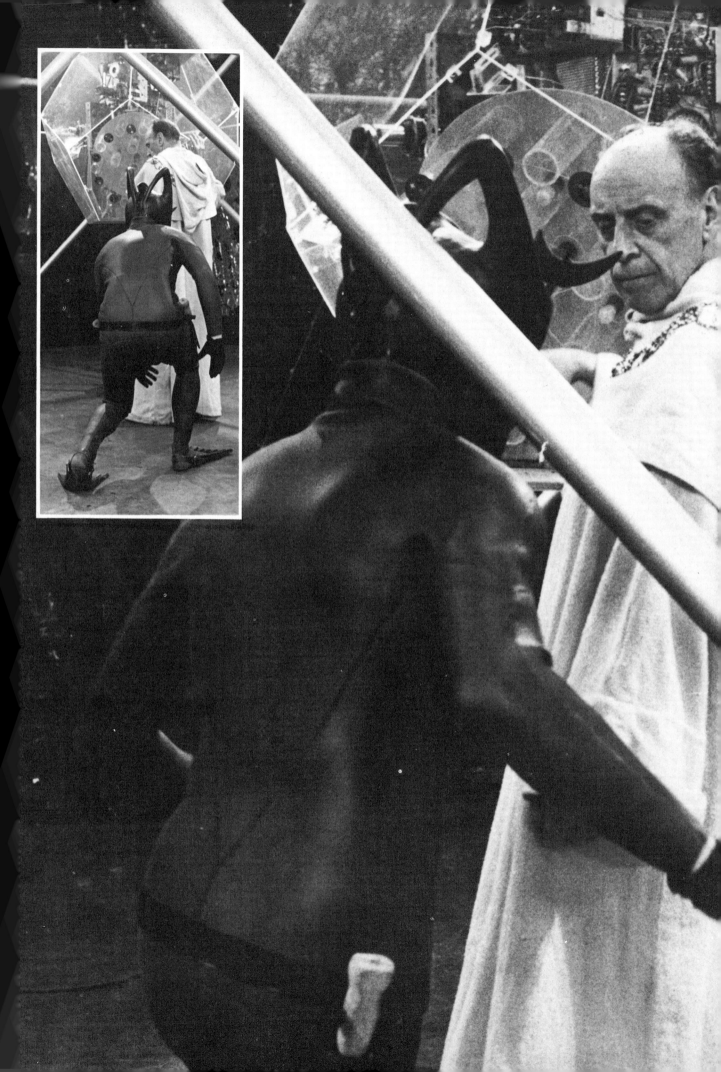

He has one of them, the remaining four having been scattered over the planet for security. Arbitan persuades the time-travellers to go in search of the keys. With them he can reprogram the Conscience to overcome the Voord's immunisation, and re-establish peace on Marinus.

Arbitan gives each of them a 'Travel Dial', a wrist-watch shaped device that permits instantaneous teleportation to the zones where the keys are hidden. They must recover the keys before the Voord seize the island.

Their first journey is to the stone city of Morphoton – an idyllic civilisation whose inhabitants apparently delight in serving others. However, Barbara is first to discover it is all a façade. A race of brain creatures rules the city, sapping the wills and minds of newcomers until they become witless slaves of the creatures.

Narrowly escaping enslavement Ian, Barbara and Susan, plus Arbitan's daughter Sabetha and her lover Altos, move on to a jungle where the vegetation is hostile. There they recover two keys from the aged scientist Darrius – one a false key, the other real.

A snowy wasteland yields the third key, but only after a desperate struggle with its guardians, the Ice Soldiers.

The fourth key proves the most difficult to locate. Reunited with the Doctor in the capital city of Millenius, Ian finds himself facing a charge of murder amidst a civilisation believing a defendant guilty until proven innocent. Only after a web of intrigue has been broken are the true culprits revealed.

On their return to the Conscience Island the travellers find the Voord in control, and Arbitan dead. Yartek himself is now the Keeper and by various threats and deceptions he prises the keys from them. Too late Yartek discovers one key to be the fake one. The Conscience is destroyed. From now on the people of Marinus must find their own answers.

**Background:** The sheer number of sets required per week made this story something of a Designer's nightmare for Raymond Cusick. Each episode brought with it a succession of new sets and new working constraints.

Part One was the most complex episode – requiring an alien beach set, the exteriors and interiors of a majestic pyramid, full side midget submarine props, a set of working miniatures, inlay shots, plus a full-size rendition of the Conscience Machine.

As with most of the *Doctor Who* stories of this period, the job of building all the special hardware and models was farmed out to the *Shawcraft* firm of prop-builders.

The other episodes were slightly easier insofar that some of the 'flats' (the walls of a set) could come from stock held at the BBC. But even here, problems arose. Proposing to use a set of stock 'rock walls' for the caves in the 'Snows of Terror' episode, Cusick discovered too late they were in fact 'stone walls', thereby requiring very, very low key lighting throughout the episode to disguise this blatant fact.

Low-key lighting and black drapes also disguised the absence of budget sufficient to afford a full set for the Brain Creatures seen in

PREVIOUS PAGES:
The murder of Arbitan, Keeper of the Conscience of Marinus (George Coulouris).

the episode 'The Velvet Web'. However, as Cusick maintained, once the audience had seen people coming and going through a stone doorway they would subconsciously assume the rest of the set to be stone as well.

Also from stock came many of the set dressings, including one latticed wall divider used in virtually every episode for a different function.

Strangely, for a *Doctor Who* story, the alien villains of the piece, the Voord, were seen only in Episode One and in half of Episode Six. Costume Supervisor Daphne Dare designed their appearance, basing their shape on a standard skin-diver's wet suit. The masks, however, were specially constructed – made from heavy-duty, vulcanised rubber and fitted by stretching them over the actors' heads so that they clamped underneath the nose and at the back of the crown.

An aspect of this story was the total absence of the Doctor from Episodes Three and Four. This stemmed from a need to give the regular cast holidays during the otherwise punishing year-long recording schedule. Throughout the Sixties various means were employed to give the cast time off, though not normally for longer than one week at a time. In 'The Aztecs' Susan appears only briefly in a filmed insert during Part Three. Similarly, in Part Two of 'The Reign of Terror' one filmed insert disguises William Russell's absence that week. And in Part Four of 'The Dalek Invasion of Earth' the back view of 'actor's double' Edmund Warwick substitutes for William Hartnell's presence in that episode.

Stock film of snowy wastelands, blizzard conditions, howling wolves, etc. enhanced the setting for the 'Snows of Terror' episode. Buying the rights to use a section from a feature film, or even an off-cut from a film, was, and remains, a standard practice open to Directors confined by the limits of budgeting. At around £5 per foot in 1964 it was not considered too expensive.

Barbara encounters the hideous Brain Creatures of Morphoton.

4 COPPER DISCS 1½" DIA WITH SPIRAL WIRE
ATTACHED, ALL COPPER FINISH
                        4/OFF

①  COPPER DISCS - 4/OFF

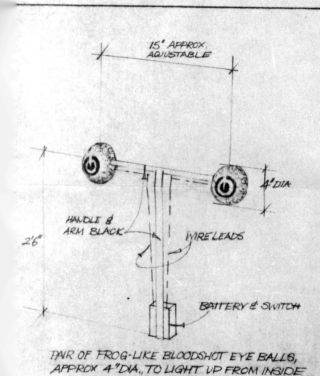

15" APPROX.
ADJUSTABLE

4"DIA.

HANDLE &
ARM BLACK

WIRE LEADS

2'6"

BATTERY & SWITCH

PAIR OF FROG-LIKE BLOODSHOT EYE BALLS,
APPROX 4"DIA., TO LIGHT UP FROM INSIDE

②  PAIR OF EYES - 1/OFF

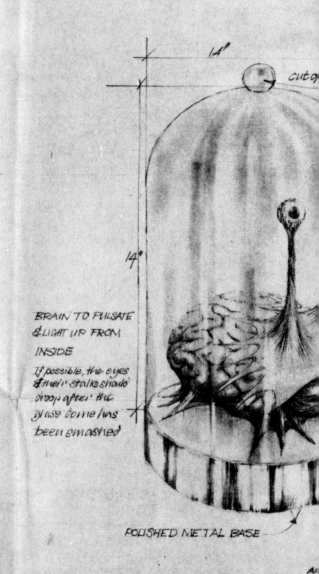

14"

cut o

14"

BRAIN TO PULSATE
& LIGHT UP FROM
INSIDE

If possible, the eyes
& their stalks should
droop after the
glass dome has
been smashed

POLISHED METAL BASE

CONSTRUCTION        PAINTERS        ARTISTS

As above, and as arranged with des

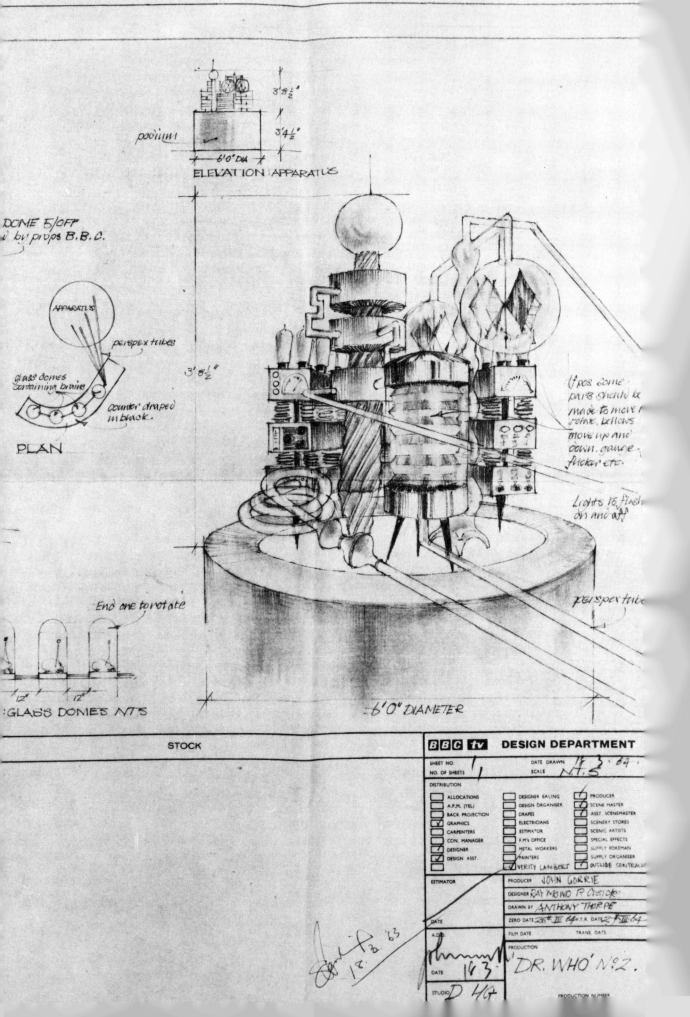

ELEVATION APPARATUS

podium

3'8½"

3'4½"

6'0" DIA

DOME 5/OFF
by props B.B.C.

APPARATUS

perspex tubes

glass domes
containing brains

counter draped
in black.

PLAN

3'8½"

If pos some
parts should be
made to move
rotate, bellows
move up and
down, gauge
flicker etc.

Lights to flash
on and off

End one to rotate

perspex tube

12"    12"

GLASS DOMES NTS

6'0" DIAMETER

perspex tube

STOCK

**BBC tv** **DESIGN DEPARTMENT**

| SHEET NO. | | DATE DRAWN | 18.3.64 |
| NO. OF SHEETS | 1 | SCALE | N.T.S |

DISTRIBUTION

| ALLOCATIONS | DESIGNER EALING | ☑ PRODUCER |
| A.P.M. (TEL) | DESIGN ORGANISER | ☑ SCENE MASTER |
| BACK PROJECTION | DRAPES | ☑ ASST. SCENEMASTER |
| ☑ GRAPHICS | ELECTRICIANS | SCENERY STORES |
| CARPENTERS | ESTIMATOR | SCENIC ARTISTS |
| CON. MANAGER | F.M's OFFICE | SPECIAL EFFECTS |
| ☑ DESIGNER | METAL WORKERS | SUPPLY FOREMAN |
| ☑ DESIGN ASST. | PAINTERS | SUPPLY ORGANISER |
| | ☑ VERITY LAMBERT | ☑ OUTSIDE CONTRACTOR |

| ESTIMATOR | | PRODUCER | JOHN GORRIE |
| | | DESIGNER | RAYMOND P CUSICK |
| | | DRAWN BY | ANTHONY THORPE |
| DATE | | ZERO DATE 26ᵗʰ III 64 V.T.R. DATE 27 III 64 |
| A.D.M. | | FILM DATE | TRANS. DATE |
| | | PRODUCTION | 'DR. WHO' Nº 2. |
| | DATE 14.3 | |
| STUDIO D 4G | | PRODUCTION NUMBER |

18.3.63

## Production Credits

Serial 'E'
Six Episodes
Black and White

| | |
|---|---|
| 'The Sea of Death' | 11 April 1964 |
| 'The Velvet Web' | 18 April 1964 |
| 'The Screaming Jungle' | 25 April 1964 |
| 'The Snows of Terror' | 2 May 1964 |
| 'Sentence of Death' | 9 May 1964 |
| 'The Keys of Marinus' | 16 May 1964 |

**Cast**

| | |
|---|---|
| Doctor Who | William Hartnell |
| Ian Chesterton | William Russell |
| Barbara Wright | Jacqueline Hill |
| Susan Foreman | Carole Ann Ford |
| | |
| Arbitan | George Coulouris |
| Arbitan's Double | John Beerbohm |
| Altos | Robin Phillips |
| Sabetha | Katherine Schofield |
| Voice of Morpho | Heron Carvic |
| Ladies in Waiting | Faith Hines, Daphne Thomas, Veronica Thornton, Sharon Young, Lynda Taylor |
| Darrius | Edmund Warwick |
| Idol | Bob Haddow |
| Hatchetman | Martin Cort |
| Vasor | Francis De Wolff |
| Ice Soldier | Michael Allaby |
| Ice Soldiers | Anthony Verner, Alan James, Peter Stenson |
| Eprin | Dougie Dean |
| Tarron | Henley Thomas |
| Larn | Michael Allaby |
| Senior Judge | Raf De La Torre |
| First Judge | Alan James |
| Second Judge | Peter Stenson |
| Kala | Fiona Walker |
| Aydan | Martin Cort |
| Eyesen | Donald Pickering |
| Guard | Alan James |
| Yartek | Stephen Dartnell |
| Voord | Martin Cort, Peter Stenson, Gordon Wales |

**Crew**

| | |
|---|---|
| Production Assistant | David Conroy |
| Assistant Floor Manager | Timothy Combe |
| Costume Supervisor | Daphne Dare |
| Make-up Supervisor | Jill Summers |
| Incidental Music | Norman Kay |
| Story Editor | David Whitaker |
| Designer | Raymond Cusick |
| Associate Producer | Mervyn Pinfield |
| Producer | Verity Lambert |
| Director | John Gorrie |

# THE SENSORITES

The Cusick Stories
Serial 'G'

**Synopsis:** The spectre of warfare fought through the mind looms up before the Doctor and his friends as they swap the bright illumination of the TARDIS for the dark, claustrophobic interior of an orbiting space rocket.

At first the companions think they have stumbled across a dead ship; the crew lies slumped over the flight deck controls, their heartbeats non-existent. Remarkably, though, the condition of the pilots – a man, Maitland, and a woman, Carol – proves only temporary. With a little help from the time-travellers they wake to full consciousness, explaining their former state as a catatonic trance induced by the inhabitants of the world they are orbiting, the Sensorites.

The Sensorites, it transpires, are a race of telepaths adept in the control of the mind. Ever since his ship approached this world – the Sense-Sphere – Maitland's crew have been subjected to telepathic assault, a process which has sent the vessel's mineralogist quite mad.

The Doctor's party are drawn unwillingly into this conflict on

Unmasked for rehearsals, the Sensorite leaders debate the arrival of their visitors.

discovering someone, or something, has removed the lock of the TARDIS – effectively stranding them aboard the rocket. Attempts to pilot the craft prove useless. The Sensorites' combined power of illusion is great enough to swamp even the Doctor's deductive abilities.

A sensitive herself, Susan is first to feel the bids by the Sensorites to make telepathic contact. They want a meeting, they intimate, and are boarding for that purpose now.

Confrontation with the two envoys is very eye-opening. Despite their gift as mental giants, the Sensorites are physically quite innocuous – small, corpulent and soft-spoken, they have extreme aversions to loud noise and darkness. These weaknesses the Doctor ruthlessly exploits in a bid to regain his lock. But the two 'warriors' explain that ever since the first Earth party came to the Sense-Sphere years ago, repaying kindness with treachery in a bid to seize control of the planet's rich stocks of the metal molybdenum, all humans are now made permanent prisoners. The Sensorites are pacifists and so cannot kill.

The Doctor, Ian, Susan and Carol travel down to the Sense-

Infuriated by the Sensorites' impertinence, the Doctor tells them exactly why they are going to return the lock of his TARDIS!

Sphere capital, with John, whom the Sensorites have offered to cure, to meet the rulers and to try and negotiate a settlement of their differences.

Though greeted with courtesy and politeness by the First and Second Elders, the intrusion of more humans onto the Sense-Sphere is covertly opposed by the City Administrator.

Ian falls victim to a disease which, for a long time, has been killing the Sensorites and which the Doctor traces to the city's water supply. Venturing into the city's underground reservoirs the Doctor finds clumps of Deadly Nightshade growing, and also a party of human survivors from the first expedition.

Led by a madman, the humans have been poisoning the water supply. With help from Susan and a recovered Ian the renegades are caught. With the wily Administrator also arrested for treason the First Elder agrees to release both the TARDIS and Maitland's ship – on condition no further human expeditions will journey to the Sense-Sphere . . .

**Background:** Written up by playwright Peter R. Newman, this story was David Whitaker's own inspiration, aiming to show that not all the alien races in the Universe were hostile killers like the Voord and the Daleks.

In consultation with Associate Producer Mervyn Pinfield, who would direct the first four episodes, Whitaker won an agreement that everything should be done to portray the Sensorites as timid, sympathetic creatures, leaving true villainy to the beast present, if mostly dormant, in the hearts of men.

Accepting this brief, Costume and Make-up Supervisors Daphne Dare and Jill Summers designed the Sensorites precisely to suggest all the above.

The fabric masks were built over an underskull frame. With no-one at the BBC at that time skilled enough in working latex rubber the masks were solid, ie: the mouths, cheeks, noses and eyes did not move. Nevertheless, by not extending the underskull over the chin, and by covering the lower part of the mask fabric in hair, enough jaw movement was permitted for the actors to convey speech with some realism.

The shape of the masks was crafted to suggest a combination of 'wise old man' with cat-like timidity, the former emphasised by the size of their skulls plus strands of wispy hair and beards, the latter by the feline expressions sculpted onto the faces, each one of which was different.

On the costume side the addition of 'Mickey Mouse' feet strove to give them both an alien and a slightly comic appearance, again emphasising the points Whitaker wanted stressed from the script about these quizzical little xenophobics.

In casting the Sensorites Mervyn Pinfield went deliberately for older, more rotund actors. An unlikely choice, many would have thought, was comedian Peter Glaze to play the role of the evil City Administrator. As it turned out the selection of Glaze (who later played a comic Doctor in a Christmas pantomime for the children's variety show *Crackerjack*) proved inspired. Even on his death, nearly twenty years later, the obituaries did not forget Glaze's role in *Doctor Who*.

Episodes Four and Five saw the turn of Jacqueline Hill (Barbara) to take a fortnight's holiday – her character being conveniently left aboard the space-craft, the sets of which are not seen again after Part Three.

While the story experienced no hiccups in production, it did cause something of a furore on its first transmission in the UK. Due to the over-running of the Wimbledon Women's Singles tennis final on 4 July, the BBC elected to postpone Episode Three until the following weekend. Reportedly the BBC switchboards were jammed with complaints most of that Saturday evening.

## Production Credits

Serial 'G'
Six Episodes
Black and White

| | |
|---|---|
| 'Strangers in Space' | 20 June 1964 |
| 'The Unwilling Warriors' | 27 June 1964 |
| | 11 July 1964 |
| 'Hidden Danger' | 18 July 1964 |
| 'Race Against Death' | 25 July 1964 |
| 'Kidnap' | 1 August 1964 |
| 'A Desperate Venture' | |

**Cast**

| | |
|---|---|
| Doctor Who | William Hartnell |
| Ian Chesterton | William Russell |
| Barbara Wright | Jacqueline Hill |
| Susan Foreman | Carole Ann Ford |
| | |
| John | Stephen Dartnell |
| Captain Maitland | Lorne Cossette |
| Carol Richmond | Ilona Rodgers |
| First Sensorite | Ken Tyllsen |
| Second Sensorite | Joe Greig |
| Third Sensorite | Peter Glaze |
| Fourth Sensorite | Arthur Newall |
| First Elder | Eric Francis |
| Second Elder | Bartlett Mullins |
| Commander | John Bailey |
| First Human | Martyn Huntley |
| Second Human | Giles Phibbs |
| Other Sensorites | Anthony Rogers |
| | Gerry Martin |

**Crew**

| | |
|---|---|
| Production Assistant | David Conroy |
| Assistant Floor Manager | Valerie McCrimmon |
| Costume Supervisor | Daphne Dare |
| Make-up Supervisor | Jill Summers |
| Incidental Music | Norman Kay |
| Story Editor | David Whitaker |
| Designer | Raymond P. Cusick |
| Associate Producer | Mervyn Pinfield |
| Producer | Verity Lambert |
| Director (1, 2, 3, 4) | Mervyn Pinfield |
| Director (5, 6) | Frank Cox |

# DANGEROUS JOURNEY

Verity Lambert, the first producer of *Doctor Who* and today one of the most successful producers in the country.

NOT GIFTED as a mind reader, Verity Lambert's initial reaction to Sydney Newman's offer to produce *Doctor Who* was one of puzzlement. With ABC she had, in several capacities, worked on a great variety of shows – light entertainment, quiz programmes, music and arts broadcasts – but never once with anything for children. Yet here she was, on the top floor of the BBC's Television Centre, being asked to shape a new serial designed to appeal to the one audience bracket of which she had no understanding.

Only as discussions settled down to specifics did some of the reasoning become clear. Sydney Newman wanted an extension of the 'kitchen sink' drama approach he had evolved to such critical acclaim with *Armchair Theatre*, one production with which Verity Lambert was well acquainted. The BBC's Children's Department, Newman felt, was still catering for only a small proportion of the nation's youngsters: the ordered few for whom parents bought *Look & Learn*, *The Eagle* or maybe even *Hotspur*. *Doctor Who* would tempt those, but more importantly also the uncatered-for majority who revelled in *Buster*, *Valiant* or the directly derivative *TV Comic*. As a bright and promising student of *Armchair Theatre* Sydney Newman felt Verity Lambert was right for the Producer's post, in spite of her distinct lack of years, being only twenty-seven at the time of her appointment.

Considering this inexperience, plus Verity Lambert's dearth of knowledge of TV technology and internal BBC procedures, Donald Wilson bestowed upon her a guardian in the guise of Mervyn Pinfield, who would be *Doctor Who*'s technical adviser under a job title of Associate Producer.

Pinfield's work in television prior to *Doctor Who* had been extensive. Very technically minded, he had been instrumental in training a lot of young Directors and PAs in the art of using the television medium to its fullest extent. For the last few years Pinfield had been based with the Langham Group, a somewhat elitist special projects body under Anthony Pellisiér charged with producing very experimental forms of drama – using techniques like inlay, overlay and split screening; for example, matting caption slide backgrounds over black drape stages. It was at the Langham studios (a BBC premises near Broadcasting House) that Mervyn Pinfield and his team hit upon the idea of pointing a video camera at its own monitor and recording the resulting 'visual feedback' (howlaround). Part of the test film they shot from these sessions (a sequence of 'rushing clouds') went into the *Doctor Who* opening title graphics, again devised by Pinfield in association with Bernard Lodge of the Graphics Unit.

(Pinfield's most remembered invention for the BBC was the Teleprompter, an easel-mounted, hand-wound scroll which bore the text read by Sports Commentators, Newsreaders and Announcers in lieu of the script. Originally titled the 'Piniprompter' the device, now termed an 'Autocue', is in use worldwide. However, being a BBC staff employee like David Whitaker, Pinfield could claim none of the potentially huge royalties due normally from such an invention.)

Mervyn Pinfield's role as Associate Producer on *Doctor Who* was agreed to be mostly in an advisory capacity. Verity Lambert would have artistic control over, and generally the casting vote in any decisions about, the programme. Pinfield would be on hand to guide her as she learned the job of producing, and to recommend ways of realising on screen any technical requirements raised in the scripts. For instance: how does one convey to an audience the notion of a ship travelling in time?

As tools to begin her new job, Sydney Newman handed Verity Lambert two documents. The first was the series format, the second was the results of a study undertaken by Cambridge University into children's perceptions of Television, as assessed from Newman's previous science fiction outing, *Pathfinders in Space*. Both proved to be valuable direction pointers.

'The format very cleverly set up those four characters to perform certain dramatic functions that were very useful for us,' says Verity Lambert. 'The Doctor was irascible, unpredictable and, as Sydney pointed out to me, his character would be very

useful if something started to get boring in a script. If that happened, or you started to get bogged down in an episode, you could always use the Doctor as a diversion. You see, it was entirely within his character to create a situation of interest either by being excessively cantankerous as an old man, or by exhibiting his somewhat childish traits.

'The Cambridge University report I read with great interest because I had no understanding of children, not having any of my own. The one thing I remember taking from that report was the recommendation about how one should present drama to children; that you don't patronise, you don't talk down. Children are as perceptive as adults really, it's just that their perception is slightly different and so there are certain things you don't deal with.

'By the time I'd finished reading the report I was fairly confident that if I, as an adult, accepted what was on that screen as being right, valid and interesting, then it would be the same for a child – provided I took out any excessive sexuality and violence. My brief was to work for 8 to 14-year-olds, the group examined in the report, not younger children where there are different problems in conveying drama.'

The limits *Doctor Who* would go in presenting 'real life drama' Verity Lambert worked out with David Whitaker once the two began collaborating on story content. An early rule-of-thumb was to avoid any extremes of emotional behaviour. Extemporised hate would not be covered, nor would the tragedy of loss. At the other end of the scale, romantic interest would only exist at a very superficial level, and certainly there would be no question of relationships forming between the TARDIS incumbents. This had to be so, Verity Lambert maintained, because of all the other elements covered in the show:

'I didn't consider overt romantic interest because *Doctor Who* was an adventure story. Also it had to be a means by which children could assimilate knowledge through watching these serials, particularly the ones set in the past.'

The cavemen story was finished and ready in script form by the time Verity Lambert arrived at the BBC, the only change from the format she had read being the shift of Susan into the role of granddaughter to the Doctor. This was at Anthony Coburn's insistence, who felt there was something 'not quite right' about an unspoken-for teenage girl travelling about the Universe with an old man. Initially Verity Lambert was resistant to this change, only in retrospect agreeing this gave Susan's character greater depth than otherwise might have been possible:

'I found it very difficult to judge that first script. I think, because I had been working on *Armchair Theatre*, I was used to a certain style of drama, so when I saw the first *Doctor Who* script my first reaction was, after the first half hour, all we were left with was a lot of hairy-chested cavemen jumping around, grunting and going "Ug". Probably had I been there at the point of commissioning I would not have chosen that story. I thought it was a very difficult and dangerous one for us to start out with. It's very hard to invest reality into people running around with clubs making funny noises. I think we were lucky to get away with it, and lucky to get a Director like Waris Hussein who managed to create this very strange quality in the cavemen that made them so interesting.'

A lot of Verity Lambert's involvement at ABC TV had been in the realm of scripts, hence in their early days together she and David Whitaker worked very closely in the selecting of *Doctor Who* stories and the nature of their content. Between four and six episodes was Verity Lambert's ideal length for a story, preferring the latter as it gave more opportunity for character development which, in her belief, audiences appreciated.

The problems encountered on the cavemen story prefaced the decision to drop Anthony Coburn's second story, 'The Robots'. *Doctor Who* demanded a certain style of writing which, in the eyes of the Production Office, the second script just did not contain.

'Tony was an exceedingly good writer, but he was not naturally a *Doctor Who* writer, and I think David felt that too. There were a lot or arguments about those first four half hours where I think it became apparent that Tony wanted to write a different type of series to the one David and I wanted. That became even more apparent when the second script came in, and so we had to drop it. In many ways that does tend to be a common occurrence on new shows when nobody has yet seen the type of programme the Producer and Story Editor have in mind.'

The push to get the first story into the can proved a very tough course indeed, especially for a fledgling Producer used to the more singular ways of commercial Television. The BBC, as a corporate body, comprised many departments and divisions, many inter-related and many, frequently, with axes to grind. Almost from its first departmental production meeting *Doctor Who* found itself the target of several wielded axes.

'We weren't liked at all to begin with, especially by the Children's Department who resented the fact that a programme aimed at 8 to 14-year-olds had been given to the Drama Group, and not to them.'

The crux of the rows centred around a belief that Sydney Newman, promoted from ITV into a very senior position and given virtual *carte blanche* to reshape the BBC's drama output, was carrying out his task by bringing in other friends and associates from ITV in place of BBC staff who felt they could equally rise to the challenges. As *Doctor Who* swung into production, envious eyes in the Children's Department studied its apparently lavish costume and set provisions, distinctly convinced that the programme was being made with an inflated budget won at the expense of cutbacks in standard children's output. What none of them chose to believe was *Doctor Who*'s initial budget of just £2,500 per episode, and that the lavish costumes and sets for the historical serials were hired out from theatrical costumiers or were hand-me-downs from previous BBC period dramas. Only in one respect was any real money spent on *Doctor Who*, and that was for the TARDIS set in Episode One, the cost of which was spread out anyway throughout the rest of the season.

92

As other departments, such as Visual Effects, joined in the unofficial boycott of *Doctor Who* (see Chapter Five), Verity Lambert, Mervyn Pinfield and their team had to fall back on ingenuity from their Designers and Directors, plus backing from Sydney Newman and Donald Wilson who both maintained great faith in the prospects of the show. This faith extended to allowing Verity Lambert considerable freedom in choosing her Directors, a key area where selecting the right type of Director was as important as finding the right sort of author.

'Sydney decided that *Doctor Who* should be a place where young people worked. I was a young Producer, and he thought it would be a good training ground for promising up-and-coming Directors as well. He felt that, on the whole, we should aim for people who had come off the BBC training course, who weren't yet ready to tackle major dramas, but who needed to cut their teeth on something demanding. So, with some limitations, I was allowed to choose new Directors whose short training films I'd seen, or who'd maybe done a couple of other jobs in serials, and get them to prove their mettle.

'Waris Hussein was a good example. I think he'd done a few *Compact*'s up to then, but he was marvellous. In all I think I only insisted on one cut to anything he did, and that was the fight between the two cavemen in the first story which ended with one of them smashing a rock down on the other's head. You didn't see it, of course, but if I remember correctly, Waris had added to the film the sound effect of a raw cabbage being crushed. I asked him to take that out, but I'm sure that was the only edit I ever insisted on from his work, which otherwise was super.

'Occasionally it was a bit hairy dealing with new Directors who'd just come off the course, so I liked to balance things by including a few established stalwarts, like Christopher Barry, whom I could rely on to be very efficient and get shows together on time. With the first Dalek one, for example, I let Richard Martin, again a new Director, do a few episodes but under the wings of Christopher who set up the serial and so, kind of, held his hand while he eased himself into the role of Director, which was good experience for him. I think Mervyn did the same with Douglas Camfield on the Lilliput story ['Planet of Giants'] we did later.'

27 September 1963 stands as the day the cameras first began rolling to record an episode of *Doctor Who*. This was 'An Unearthly Child', the series opener whose eerie prologue, the camera tracking around the Victorian buttresses and stairwells of the 76 Totter's Lane junkyard, was accompanied by a playing of the full 1' 18" title music. Composed by Ron Grainer and arranged by Delia Derbyshire and other members of the BBC Radiophonic Workshop, this music started life as an idea in the back of Verity Lambert's mind.

'I wanted something that was melodic but yet didn't sound like any conventional grouping of instruments. In other words, I didn't want anything recognisable used at all. Initially I happened to be watching a monitor at the BBC on which was an item about a group of French musicians who played their music on glass tubes. It struck me as wonderful stuff, so I got in touch and tried to get them to do the music for *Doctor Who*, but they just didn't have the time.

'So then I had an idea that if I went to a composer who wrote very tuneful music, but asked him to work electronically rather than with instruments, I might end up with what I wanted, which was music the ear could relate to, rather than *musique concrète* which was the other sort of electronic music being done at the time.

'I went to Ron Grainer, who had written themes for programmes like *Maigret* and *Steptoe and Son*, and asked him how he would feel trying to achieve a melody electronically. He jumped at it.

'I can't remember now if the titles came before the music, or the music before the titles. I would tend to think the titles came first as it was usual to show a composer something of what you were envisaging. Interestingly enough, the Monday after the first episode was shown, a film company rang us up to ask how the titles had been done. For me that was vindication for the disagreements I'd had with Sydney Newman and Donald Wilson, both of whom saw the music and titles after they'd been done and said they didn't like them. In fact Sydney said, "You've got to change them", which I refused to do.'

The row over the titles was just one of several run-ins Verity Lambert had with her two department heads in the early months, particularly over the first episode. Strangely enough these stemmed not from any hostility towards *Doctor Who* the concept – all three were thoroughly supportive of the format – only from reservations Wilson and Newman had about the way Verity Lambert and David Whitaker were interpreting their prodigy.

Viewing the pilot episode Newman and Wilson were distinctly unhappy. Not only was production somewhat slipshod – with cameras crashing into scenery, sound effects drowning out voices, etc – but the whole dramatic structure was wrong in their eyes too. Coburn's script stated that Susan came from the forty-ninth century: too precise a reference for a series modelling itself on mystery. The Doctor was heftily criticised for being almost malevolent in his attitude towards the school teachers – too much of William Hartnell's 'hard-nosed' image was shining through. The result was a 'carpeting' for the entire production team and an explicit instruction to go back, do it again, and get it right.

Three weeks on from 27 September, 'An Unearthly Child' was rerecorded, with only the model and film footage being re-used from the pilot. This time around Waris Hussein used a full complement of four cameras instead of the two he had opted to use in the pilot, having expressed a preference then to experiment with 'moving camera technique'.

This version did receive approval and the weekly cycle of episode recording commenced in earnest. But a new row was just around the corner.

Both David Whitaker and Verity Lambert had been captivated by Terry Nation's Dalek story right from the moment they saw the first 'treatment' (story idea). The script was commissioned quickly to replace Coburn's dropped 'The Robots' story and thereby maintain the balance between historical and futuristic adventures, and production was scheduled and slotted to follow on a week later from 'The Tribe of Gum'. A fortnight later Lambert and Whitaker got summoned to the Head of Serials' office to discuss 'The Daleks' . . .

'Donald Wilson hated it. He called David and I in and said he had read the scripts and thought they were terrible. He didn't like the idea, he didn't like the writing . . . In fact he virtually told us we shouldn't do it. David and I then had to tell him we didn't have any choice because at that time there were no other futuristic stories ready. We needed to alternate between the past and the future, and while we had two good historical scripts in, none of the writers David had commissioned had yet produced anything set in the future which we could use.

'However, in fairness to him, after we'd done "The Daleks" and it had been so successful, Donald Wilson said to me, "I clearly don't know anything about this series, and you do, so I'll leave you alone", which was nice of him.'

The first episode of *Doctor Who* was transmitted on Saturday 23 November 1963, a historic day marking also the aftermath of President Kennedy's assassination. So disrupted were the TV schedules that day, with viewers switching between channels to glean the latest news from America, that Verity Lambert won permission to have 'An Unearthly Child' rescreened the following Saturday, before 'The Cave of Skulls' (the story's second episode) to enable more balanced viewer ratings to be established.

Production was mid-way through 'The Daleks' when the first survey results came through. The figures were promising, but not spectacular, and that was all the ammunition the next round of opponents needed to fire a broadside across *Doctor Who*'s bows. And this time they almost succeeded . . .

'There was a big wave of resistance to *Doctor Who* all through the BBC after we first went out. Aside from the Children's Department, the Design Department, in the early weeks, were enraged by us; not the Designers themselves, who were absolutely terrific to us, but the people who ran it who were often extremely unhelpful.

'The first episode was very popular, but the show didn't suddenly take off – which any programme doesn't in four weeks. Anyway I was told it had to finish in thirteen weeks. The BBC suddenly decided it wanted to stop *Doctor Who*. I don't know who it was made the decision, I was only a very junior Producer. I was called in and told the show was too expensive and was stretching facilities far too greatly for a children's programme.'

Painstakingly Verity Lambert explained to her superiors the impracticality of a thirteen week, quarter-year season; the four part cavemen story was in the can, the seven part Dalek serial was under way, and they were committed to running 'Marco Polo', also seven episodes in length, giving a grand total of eighteen weeks in all. Accepting the logic of this situation the matter was held over for further review at a later Department Head meeting. But by that time, history had been made.

'During that interim period *Doctor Who* just took off with the Daleks in a way that none of us could have imagined, and after that there was no more discussion about it coming off the air.

'However, the point is that for quite a long time nobody really wanted to know about *Doctor Who* outside Sydney and Donald. I thought this was quite a plus actually, because we were able to get away with murder during the beginning, in some ways doing things that on paper looked very expensive but in reality balanced out over the year we were scheduled.'

Unquestionably *Doctor Who*'s biggest champions at the BBC were Sydney Newman and Donald Wilson, the former in particular nursing strong personal convictions about the potential power of its semi-educational qualities. The early historical serials, typified by 'Marco Polo', more than lived up to his expectations,

History in the making: the dramatic first appearance of the Daleks in the episode 'The Survivors'. When he first saw the Daleks Sydney Newman was furious, claiming that Lambert had betrayed the whole concept of *Doctor Who*.

*Above:* The initial production illustration for the Sand Beast on Dido, later modified in greater detail when the go-ahead had been given. *Below:* The final version, worked out with Christopher Barry and Verity Lambert once the budget had been agreed upon ('The Rescue').

OPPOSITE
*Top left:* The abortive attempt to bury a Dalek in 'The Chase'; *Top right:* The Daleks in the winding metal corridors of their city on Skaro ('The Daleks'); *Below:* The end of the evil mutants? ('The Daleks')

Ray Cusick's illustration of the mutant which dwells within the Dalek machine: the creature proved too expensive to make.

The backdrop painting of the petrified forest on Skaro in which the TARDIS lands ('The Daleks'). *Inset from top to bottom:* The model set of the forest, first seen at the end of 'The Tribe of Gum' story; the full-size set ('The Daleks'); part of the swamp set from 'The Daleks', including the latex 'octopus' creature which devoured the Thal, Elyon (note the air hose for the rubber ring on the left of the picture).

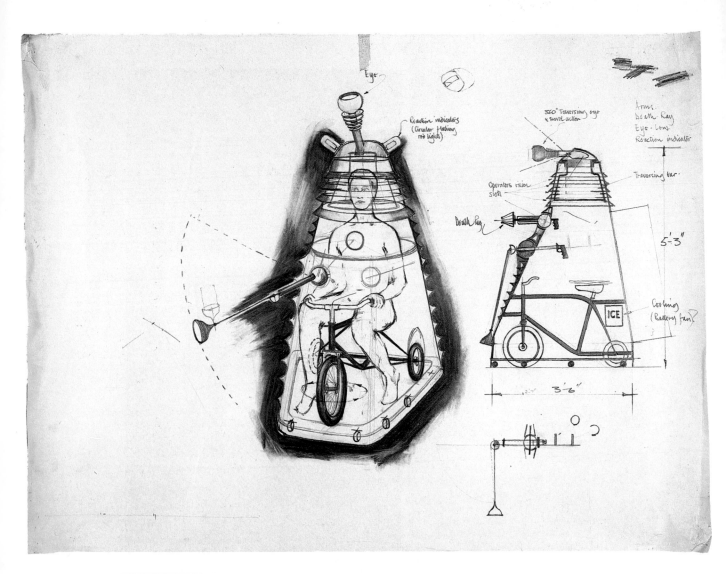

*Top:* Production drawing of the Dalek, presented to Verity Lambert and Christopher Barry. The drawing shows the tricycle motive system, two hand mechanisms, and a gun aperture, mounted above the midriff. The base is squarer in design, and an ice box is installed inside the machine to keep the operator cool. *Below:* Part of the scenic backdrop of the Sensorites' city ('The Sensorites').

OPPOSITE
*Top:* The initial sketch for the flight deck of Captain Maitland's ship; *Below:* The flight deck as realised on screen, and the Doctor's encounter with the Sensorites on board Maitland's ship ('The Sensorites').

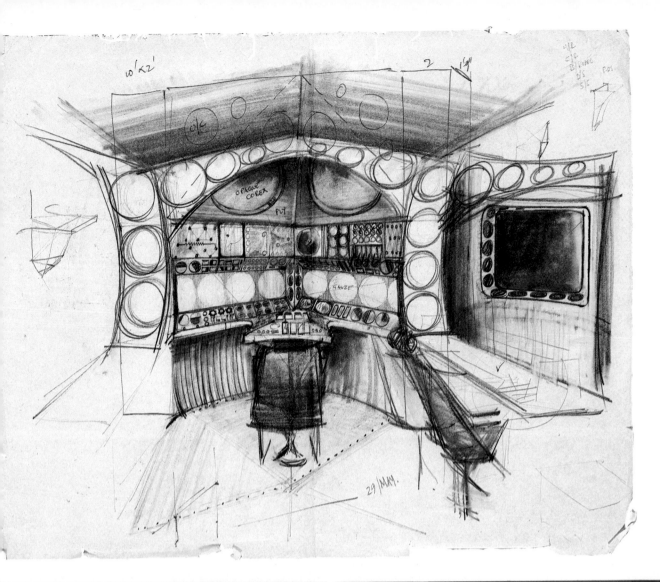

*Top:* Barbara, Susan and Ian enjoy
the apparent luxury offered them
in the City of Morphoton; *Below:*
The grim reality of the Velvet Web
('The Keys of Marinus').

drawing much critical praise from school teachers and parents as transmission stimulated children's interest in the periods of history under view.

On the futuristic stories, however, things were vastly different. With the imminent launch of BBC 2 less than six months away Sydney Newman saw little of *Doctor Who* after the pilot episodes had been approved until, at home on a Saturday afternoon, he watched the first episode featuring the Dalek machines. His reaction to them was explosive, and on Monday morning Verity Lambert was hastily summoned to his office. Newman himself recounts what transpired:

'The scene went something like this when I demanded her presence in my office:

**Me:** "I told you there were to be no bug-eyed monsters in *Doctor Who*."

**Verity:** "Honestly Sydney, they are not because . . ."

**Me:** "You've betrayed the whole concept. This is a children's series . . ."

**Verity:** "Sydney, listen. The Daleks . . ."

**Me:** "Jesus, bug-eyed monsters, cheap-jade sci-fi rubbish . . . BEMs . . ."

**Verity (shouting):** "*They are not!* There's a brain inside those metal casings . . ."

'And then Verity explained that these Daleks were so advanced in their technology, that their brains were so large and their bodies so atrophied, they needed the casings to allow them to move. "Uh huh," said I. I was not easily pacified but the show had already been aired.'

Newman's anger eventually subsided, mollified in the main by the overwhelming hit the Daleks made with the public that so proved Verity Lambert and David Whitaker's instincts correct again. Like Donald Wilson before, Newman accepted the strength of the 'Dalek Factor' and agreed to let Verity Lambert handle *Doctor Who* her way after that, even though it meant his sacrificing part of the ideals he had intended the show to represent. With the single exception of 'Planet of Giants' (née 'The Miniscules'), a story Newman virtually insisted be done, no other adventure attempted to couch its storyline within a 'Let's look at the wonders of technology/nature/medicine/etc' learning process. The aliens very definitely had taken over.

The forefronting of the *Doctor Who* monsters, in the wake of the Daleks, was a development which pleased Verity Lambert in that it virtually guaranteed constant press interest in the programme. As each new creature was unveiled so Fleet Street ran copious feature articles, often full page, to highlight what they hoped would be the next 'big thing'. But desirable though all this was, it never detracted from Verity Lambert's basic belief that the underlying strength of the series lay in its four principal artists, all of whom she thought developed the most realistic inter-relationships ever forged in a science fiction series, spearheaded, of course, by William Hartnell's magnetic interpretation of the Doctor.

'I thought William Hartnell played the part marvellously. He got everything into the character that I wanted. He was lovable at times, he was completely irritating at times, he could be quite frightening at times and, above all, which is why I think the kids related to him, he was so totally anti-establishment. Children related to him so much because they saw in him an adult who behaved in the way that they did. He wasn't perfect.'

In rationalising these qualities Verity Lambert saw two of William Hartnell's previous roles which suggested he might be suitable for the character she had in mind. The first was *The Army Game* in which Hartnell played his traditional hard-nut part as Sergeant-Major Bullimore. The second, and less obvious, was Lindsay Anderson's film *This Sporting Life* where Hartnell took the role of an ageing rugby talent scout; a somewhat sad and reflective character who looked back with fondness on his years in the game. Combining these two traits, Verity Lambert felt, would give the Doctor the essential dichotomy between the imperious master of his ship, which the Doctor thought he was, and the quirky, unpredictable old salt, which he truly was. Other candidates for the Doctor included established character actors like Leslie French and Cyril Cusack, either or whom, Lambert concurs, could have interpreted the part as well, albeit differently.

Cyril Cusack for example, on the strength of his previous performances, would have made the Doctor a gentle figure, possibly more in tune with Patrick Troughton's rendering some years later.

'It's very difficult to explain how you cast people because it's really to do with instinct. You just get a feeling that one actor is going to give you that certain something which you're looking for. Bill did, and right from the start he was thrilled by the part. There was no feeling whatsoever that it was a come-down, his doing a programme for children. If anything, he was a little nervous about his ability to sustain so demanding a role for fifty-two weeks.

'William Russell I had always, always liked as an actor. He had been Sir Lancelot, which was a heroic character, but what we wanted with Ian was someone resonant that the public would respond to. Russ looked like a school master, although not quite in the stereotype of a middle class school teacher. He had a sense of humour about him and, I suppose, a kind of lesser quirkiness that made him very natural in the part.

'Jacqueline was the same. I'd known her, and her husband Alan Rakoff, for a long time and as I began searching for someone to play Barbara I just found myself thinking about her. She was intelligent, attractive, but you believed again she could be a school teacher.

'With Susan we auditioned quite a few people before Carole Ann came in. But she was just so bubbly and so vivacious, and she looked so young despite being well over eighteen, that there was something almost right for her in the part. And she could scream as well . . . Ideally we might have preferred a juvenile actress, but with the restrictions on the hours children can work in Television we knew we couldn't do it that way.'

Ironically it was Susan's supposed age of around fifteen that so landed *Doctor Who* in more hot water when the two part 'Edge of Destruction' story went out. Featured in that episode was the infamous sequence where a concussed Susan menaces Ian, and then Barbara, with a pair of sharply-pointed scissors. The repercussions of those scenes served to remind Verity Lambert of her responsibilities as Producer of a show aimed at youngsters.

'The full weight of the Children's Department came down on us for that scene and, in retrospect, I realised I had made a mistake letting that go through. It might have been dubious to have had any of the characters holding the scissors, but because it was the child of the foursome doing it, that made it an even bigger mistake, which I accepted, putting it down totally to inexperience on my behalf. I had to write a letter of apology to the Children's Department about the incident, which hadn't done our already bad standing with them any good at all.'

That was the last of the major rows which seemed to haunt the Production Office throughout its formative first year, but it was a sad indictment that *Doctor Who* never won full respectability as a serious drama programme within the Corporation. For most of its life, and certainly for its early years, it was either too outspoken to be a children's show, but not high-brow enough to be considered as adult entertainment. Success was found in a limbo area mid-way between BBC dubiousness and general public enthusiasm.

'I was mainly concerned with making something that children could enjoy and not feel that this was a special programme for them, avoiding all the twee and awful things people normally put into children's programmes. I wanted them to have a programme they could say they watched simply because they liked and enjoyed it.'

# PLANET OF GIANTS

The Cusick Stories
Serial 'J'

**Synopsis:** As the TARDIS slips forward in time from the French Revolution a freak accident causes the main doors to swing open briefly during materialisation. Uncertain as to the cause the Doctor is even more worried about the possible effects. An attempt to use the scanner to survey their new landing point fails; the screen explodes almost as if, the Doctor muses, the images outside were too great to fill the picture area . . .

Worried, the time-travellers venture out only to discover the ship has landed in a narrow, rocky gully strewn with rocks and boulders. Cautiously setting out to explore the many winding canyons debouching from their landing point, a host of nightmarish apparitions greet their progress. Barbara finds the carcass of a huge snake, Susan and Ian stumble across a mound of eggs guarded by a giant ant (fortunately also dead), while the Doctor mutters darkly about some intelligence having carved these channels in the rocks, but for what purpose?

The terrible truth dawns with one further discovery – a huge poster for 'Night Scented Stock' pierced through with a huge, wooden mast and next to it a giant, half-open matchbox. To Ian's suggestion that it must all be part of some exhibition Susan replies with the more plainly obvious answer – these things have not been made larger, the time-travellers have become smaller. They are all now less than one inch in height. The TARDIS has landed amid the clefts of a crazy-paved footpath.

Stuck in this predicament the four travellers become embroiled in a drama unfolding in the house nearby. Here a scientist, Smithers, has developed an insecticide, DN6, backed by a ruthless speculator named Forester. But tests by a Government inspector, Farrow, have revealed the pesticide is lethal to all insect life, and for this reason production must stop. With a lot of money at stake Forester cannot agree, and cold-bloodedly murders Farrow.

Witnesses to this crime, the time-travellers, already having seen DN6's effects on the garden's insect population, must try to alert the Police. But what would be an easy operation at normal size proves an exercise in wits and survival thanks to their Lilliputian sizes. A domestic cat becomes a deadly predator, the drain pipe demands a feat of mountain climbing to scale it, and waste water from a kitchen sink thunders down on Susan and the Doctor with the force of a tidal wave.

Added to these problems, their voices are too squeaky and high-pitched for the telephone operator to hear even after the Doctor's crew have managed to lift a telephone receiver from its rest. Luckily, however, the local village operator's suspicions are raised and her policeman husband comes to the scene, where he arrests Forester just in time to prevent him killing Smithers as well.

Forging a way back to the TARDIS, Barbara, who had fallen ill through touching some DN6-impregnated seeds, is restored to full health when the ship dematerialises, the time-travellers returning to full size in the process.

**Background:** Although given the honour of being the opening story of *Doctor Who*'s second season this serial was originally scheduled to be part of the first. Indeed, the idea dated way back to Sydney Newman's original brief about the series, as handed to Donald Wilson, where he expressed a wish to see a show done with an everyday garden made to appear every bit as hostile as an alien planet.

Bearing an original working title of 'The Miniscules', the idea of the TARDIS crew stranded in a giant house and garden was handed to Louis Marks for fleshing out with a plot. Searching for inspiration, Marks remembered a very disturbing and bestselling book of the period called *Silent Spring* by Rachel Carson, which discussed the potential knock-on effects to the ecology of over-using insecticides.

Combining the two ideas produced a four part storyline which went into studio production during August 1964. Due to some highly complex, and to a degree innovative, technical requirements, the job of directing went to Associate Producer Mervyn Pinfield for Episodes One to Three, and to rapidly

The elaborate glass shot of the house from 'Planet of Giants'. The ground floor of the house is a set, and the first floor is a glass painting. Flowers in the foreground hide the glass frame.

up-and-coming PA Douglas Camfield, making his debut as a *Doctor Who* Director on Episode Four.

The cost of this story was very high, not least for the time, materials and manpower needed to build the 'giant' sets and props (the sink, the telephone, the briefcase, the lab bench, etc.), all of which had to be robust enough for the regular cast to clamber around.

Technically the production had to be able to cater for precisely lined-up inlay shots, half-silvered mirror shots, glass shots and back-projections to overcome the great hurdle of having the travellers and the 'giants' in the same shots.

Even the audio aspect was not neglected. To demonstrate how sound patterns and perceptions change with size Sound Mixer Alan Fogg pre-recorded several segments of specially speeded up or slowed down soundtrack to show how, respectively, a tiny voice sounds to a giant, and vice versa.

Only when all four episodes were completed did Verity Lambert express doubts. The miniature scenes were fine. What flagged, she felt, was the 'Tales of Scotland Yard' surrounding story which appeared so out of place in *Doctor Who*.

In the end she made the decision to combine Episodes Three

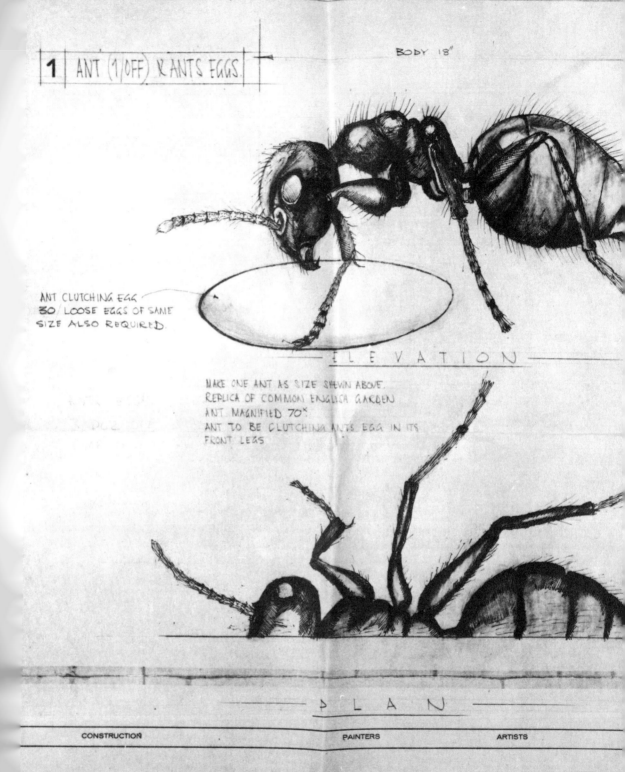

1 | ANT (1/OFF) & ANTS EGGS

BODY 18"

ANT CLUTCHING EGG
30 LOOSE EGGS OF SAME
SIZE ALSO REQUIRED.

E L E V A T I O N

MAKE ONE ANT AS SIZE SHEWN ABOVE.
REPLICA OF COMMON ENGLISH GARDEN
ANT MAGNIFIED 70×
ANT TO BE CLUTCHING ANTS EGG IN ITS
FRONT LEGS

P L A N

CONSTRUCTION          PAINTERS          ARTISTS

AS ABOVE & BY ARRANGEMENT WITH DES

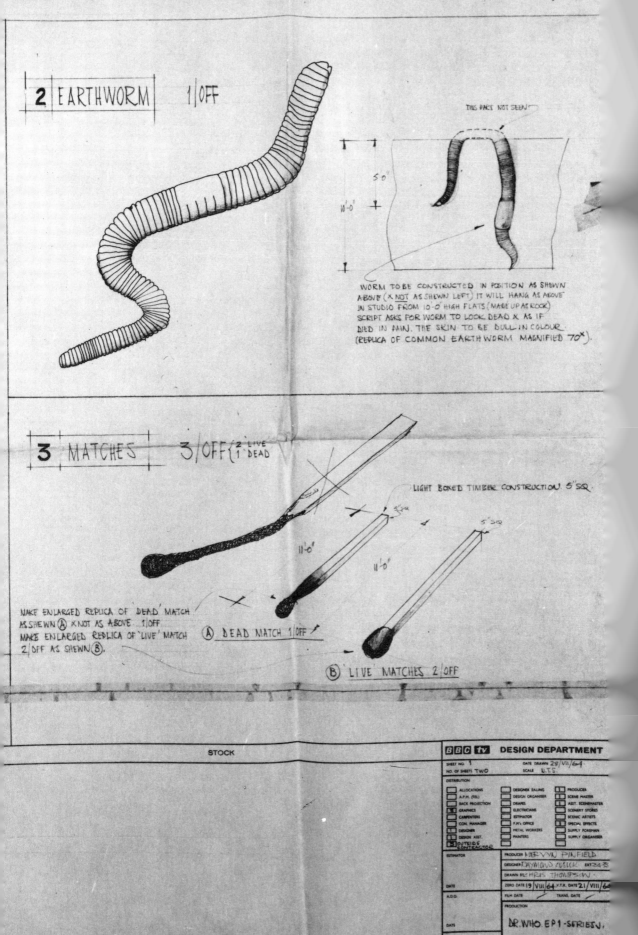

**2** EARTHWORM    1/OFF

THIS PACE NOT SEEN

5'·0"

11'·0"

WORM TO BE CONSTRUCTED IN POSITION AS SHEWN
ABOVE (✗ NOT AS SHEWN LEFT) IT WILL HANG AS ABOVE
IN STUDIO FROM 10'·0" HIGH FLATS (MADE UP AS ROCK)
SCRIPT ASKS FOR WORM TO LOOK DEAD ✗ AS IF
DIED IN PAIN. THE SKIN TO BE DULL IN COLOUR.
(REPLICA OF COMMON EARTHWORM MAGNIFIED 70ˣ).

**3** MATCHES    3/OFF { 2 LIVE
                        1 DEAD

LIGHT BOXED TIMBER CONSTRUCTION. 5" SQ.

11'·0"

5" SQ

11'·0"

5" SQ

MAKE ENLARGED REPLICA OF 'DEAD' MATCH
AS SHEWN Ⓐ ✗ NOT AS ABOVE 1/OFF
MAKE ENLARGED REPLICA OF 'LIVE' MATCH
2/OFF AS SHEWN Ⓑ.

Ⓐ DEAD MATCH 1/OFF

Ⓑ LIVE MATCHES 2/OFF

STOCK

**BBC tv   DESIGN DEPARTMENT**

| SHEET NO. 1 | | DATE DRAWN 28/VII/64 |
| NO. OF SHEETS TWO | | SCALE N.T.S. |

DISTRIBUTION

| | | |
|---|---|---|
| ALLOCATIONS | DESIGNER EALING | PRODUCER |
| A.F.M. (TEL) | DESIGN ORGANISER | SCENE MASTER |
| BACK PROJECTION | DRAPES | ASST. SCENEMASTER |
| GRAPHICS | ELECTRICIANS | SCENERY STORES |
| CARPENTERS | ESTIMATOR | SCENIC ARTISTS |
| CON. MANAGER | F.M's OFFICE | SPECIAL EFFECTS |
| DESIGNER | METAL WORKERS | SUPPLY FOREMAN |
| DESIGN ASST. | PAINTERS | SUPPLY ORGANISER |
| OUTSIDE CONTRACTOR | | |

| ESTIMATOR | PRODUCER MERVYN PINFIELD |
| | DESIGNER RAYMOND CUSICK EXT 2435 |
| | DRAWN BY CHRIS THOMPSON |
| DATE | ZERO DATE 19/VII/64 V.T.R. DATE 21/VIII/64 |
| A.D.O. | FILM DATE     TRANS. DATE |
| | PRODUCTION |
| DATE | DR. WHO. EP 1 - SERIES J. |
| STUDIO T.C.4 | PRODUCTION NUMBER 2174 |

and Four together, losing one whole episode entirely to tighten up on the drama.

By Summer 1964 the decision had been made to extend *Doctor Who*'s life by another season, which meant having a new series ready to start screening by the autumn of that year. *Doctor Who*'s studio recording schedule for 1963/64 was a full year anyway, so, to buy them more time Verity Lambert won permission for *Doctor Who* to take its transmission break after 'The Reign of Terror'. This gave them not so much a production holiday, more like two serials 'in the can' for season two (up to and including the rapidly commissioned 'The Dalek Invasion of Earth') that could be recorded during season one's contractual period.

## Production Credits

Serial 'J'
Three Episodes
Black and White

| | |
|---|---|
| 'Planet of Giants' | 31 October 1964 |
| 'Dangerous Journey' | 7 November 1964 |
| 'Crisis' | 14 November 1964 |

### Cast

| | |
|---|---|
| Doctor Who | William Hartnell |
| Ian Chesterton | William Russell |
| Barbara Wright | Jacqueline Hill |
| Susan Foreman | Carole Ann Ford |
| | |
| Forester | Alan Tilvern |
| Farrow | Frank Crawshaw |
| Smithers | Reginald Barrett |
| Hilda Rowse | Rosemary Johnson |
| Bert Rowse | Fred Ferris |

### Crew

| | |
|---|---|
| Production Assistant | Norman Stewart |
| Assistant Floor Managers | Val McCrimmon, Dawn Robertson |
| Costume Supervisor | Daphne Dare |
| Make-up Supervisor | Sonia Markham |
| Sound Mixer | Alan Fogg |
| Incidental Music | Dudley Simpson |
| Story Editor | David Whitaker |
| Designer | Raymond P. Cusick |
| Associate Producer | Mervyn Pinfield |
| Producer | Verity Lambert |
| Director (1, 2) | Mervyn Pinfield |
| Directors (3) | Douglas Camfield |

PREVIOUS PAGE:
The blueprints for the giant props used in 'Planet of Giants'. This was the last *Doctor Who* story for which Syndey Newman was directly responsible.

# THE RESCUE

The Cusick Stories
Serial 'L'

**Synopsis:** Having said farewell to Susan, the Doctor has moved the TARDIS on again, bringing it to rest in a cave somewhere on the planet Dido.

Leaving the Doctor alone with his thoughts Ian and Barbara go outside to explore. Emerging from the cave they encounter the masked form of Koquillion, who bids them to fetch the Doctor at once. But as Ian goes back to comply Koquillion uses his jewelled weapon to cause an avalanche, sealing up the cave. Retreating from the strange creature Barbara loses her balance and tumbles over a cliff.

Coming to, Barbara finds she is in the cabin of a wrecked spacecraft from Earth. She has been rescued by a young castaway named Vicki.

Vicki tells her that when the ship landed, the crew were invited to a meeting by the local inhabitants. Her father and all the others, bar one, were killed. She only escaped because she was ill at the time and had remained behind. The other survivor, Bennett, crawled back and has since lain a cripple. Now Koquillion claims

OVERLEAF:
Construction drawings of the wall carvings in and around the Didonian Hall of Judgement. They bear a striking ressemblance to Koquillion.

107

SCALE 1½ e

7' X 7' JABLITE PANELS - TWO TO BE MADE

ONE WITH HOLES AS SHOWN ON ACCOMPANYING SHEET -

ONE WITH HOLES TO BE PAINTED AS DARK GREENY HELED MARBLE TYPE ROCK

THE OTHER DULL GOLD AND BRONZE -

| CONSTRUCTION | PAINTERS | ARTISTS |
|---|---|---|

SPECIAL EFFECTS DRAW

SHAWCRAFT MODELS (UXBR

DETAILS AS ABOVE AND AS

OWEST LEVEL —

— 1 INCH —

— 2 INCHES —

— 3 INCHES —

SCALE – HALF
ACTUAL
SIZE.

18" X 18" JABLITE SQUARES WITH MONSTERS HEAD WITH RING IN MOUTH
FOUR TO BE MADE — ONE MUST HAVE RING TO WORK LOOSE AND TO COME AWAY IN ACTORS HAND —

STOCK

OUTSIDE CONTRACT —

D —

WITH DESIGNER —

| **BBC tv** | **DESIGN DEPARTMENT** | |
|---|---|---|
| SHEET NO. 2 , | DATE DRAWN 23 NOV 64. | |
| NO. OF SHEETS | SCALE +1/A/S + ½" | |

DISTRIBUTION | | | 12

| | | | | | |
|---|---|---|---|---|---|
| ☐ ALLOCATIONS | ☐ DESIGNER EALING | 2 PRODUCER | | | |
| ☐ A.P.M. (TEL) | ☐ DESIGN ORGANISER | 2 SCENE MASTER | | | |
| ☐ BACK PROJECTION | ☐ DRAPES | 2 ASST. SCENEMASTER | | | |
| 2 GRAPHICS | ☐ ELECTRICIANS | ☐ SCENERY STORES | | | |
| ☐ CARPENTERS | 2 ESTIMATOR | ☐ SCENIC ARTISTS | | | |
| ☐ CON. MANAGER | ☐ F.M's OFFICE | ☐ SPECIAL EFFECTS | | | |
| ☐ DESIGNER | ☐ METAL WORKERS | ☐ SUPPLY FOREMAN | | | |
| ☐ DESIGN ASST. | ☐ PAINTERS | ☐ SUPPLY ORGANISER | | | |
| ☐ | ☐ | 2 OUTSIDE | | | |

| ESTIMATOR | PRODUCER CHRIS BARRY |
|---|---|
| H/Warren | DESIGNER RAYMOND P. CUSICK EXT 2435 |
| | DRAWN BY CHRIS THOMPSON |
| DATE 23-11-64 | ZERO DATE 3RD DEC V.T.R. DATE 4TH DEC |
| A.D.O. | FILM DATE          TRANS. DATE |
| J.Small | PRODUCTION |
| DATE 23/11/64 | DR. WHO. |
| | SERIES 'L' |
| STUDIO R1V.1. | EP Nº I   2375 |
| | PRODUCTION NUMBER 2375 |

he is protecting them from the wrath of his people. Vicki is praying that the rescue ship she knows is on its way will arrive in time to save them all.

Reunited with the Doctor, Ian is trying to find another exit from the cave along a narrow ledge above a chasm. Accidentally he touches a staple set into the wall. A hidden mechanism activates, ejecting a series of sharp knife blades threatening to push him from the ledge. Down below the roar of a sand creature can be heard.

Luckily the Doctor remembers, from a previous visit, how to deal with the trap and they escape. They pass a stone doorway in the tunnel wall, but by-pass it in favour of a more obvious way out.

Introduced by Vicki, Barbara makes a reluctant promise to Bennett not to oppose Koquillion. She stays behind while Vicki goes to replenish the water bottles, but when the girl returns to the ship Barbara notices her being pursued by the sand creature. Grabbing a flare gun she shoots the creature, learning too late that the animal was a tame vegetarian and Vicki's pet. The Doctor and Ian hear the shot and come to the rocket. In the meantime Koquillion emerges from the tunnel door.

The Doctor decides to talk to Bennett in his cabin, but when the man tells him to go away he forces open the door – only to find a tape recorder and an escape hatch door in the floor. Alone the Doctor leaves the ship, goes back to the tunnel and enters the chamber behind the stone door. There he meets Koquillion.

The figure is unmasked as Bennett. He confesses that he killed a man on board the space ship and so would have been tried on his return to Earth. With the rocket's armaments he rigged up an explosive which killed both the crew and the people of Dido. He intends to take Vicki (who knew nothing of his crimes) back to Earth so that she will support his testimony. He attacks the Doctor, but two Didonians enter, and in terror Bennett backs away and falls over the ledge.

The TARDIS takes off, this time with a new passenger on board – Vicki.

**Background:** As mentioned before, *Doctor Who*'s cast and studio teams took a break after recording the preceding story, 'The Dalek Invasion of Earth'. That finished one year of *Doctor Who* production, the length originally agreed by Sydney Newman and Donald Wilson.

In the intervening period, of course, the Daleks had changed the face and destiny of the show forever. Mid-way through the production year Verity Lambert, Mervyn Pinfield and David Whitaker knew they had had a second season approved by delighted BBC Television Controllers. The only big question now was who would stay on.

Of the Production trio only Verity Lambert elected to remain. Mervyn Pinfield, feeling he had done his job overcoming the show's technical worries and acting as adviser to Verity Lambert, wanted to return to the more active area of Directing. David Whitaker, heavily involved in the floodtide of Dalekmania, chose

Koquillion, the 'Powerful Enemy', and Vicki, the Doctor's new companion (Maureen O'Brien).

110

to leave the BBC to concentrate full time on lucrative freelance projects looming with Terry Nation.

From the cast only Carole Ann Ford intimated a wish to leave, somewhat worried at the prospect of being typecast as a 'screaming teenager'.

Reshaping for Season Two, Newman and Wilson felt confident enough in Verity Lambert not to fill Mervyn Pinfield's vacant seat. Able to choose his own successor David Whitaker offered the Script Editor's seat to his long-time friend and colleague Dennis Spooner.

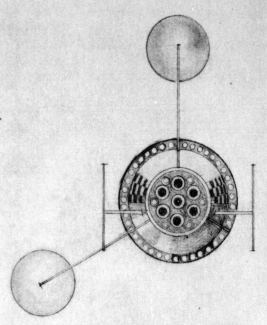

REAR ELEVATION OF SHIP.

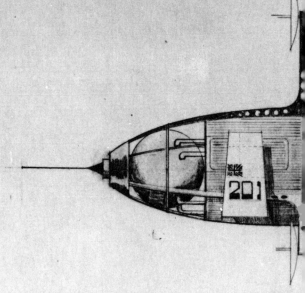

SIDE ELEVATION OF S

DETAIL OF LETTERING ACTUAL SIZE

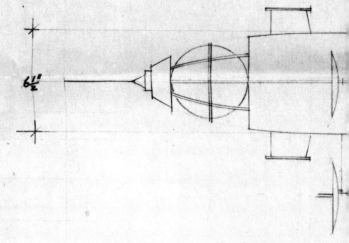

PLAN OF S

OVER-ALL LEN

| CONSTRUCTION | PAINTERS | ARTISTS |
|---|---|---|

SPECIAL EFFECTS DRAWING - OUTSIDE CONTRACT —
SHAWCRAFT MODELS (UXBRIDGE) LTD. —
DETAILS AS ABOVE AND AS DISCUSSED WITH DESIGNER—

SHEET 1 OF

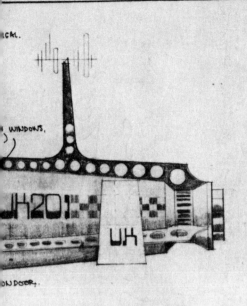

ACTUAL SIZE

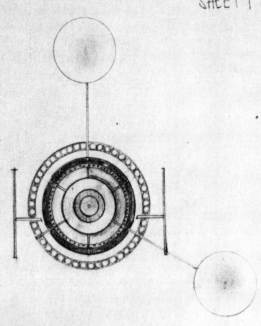

FRONT ELEVATION OF SHIP

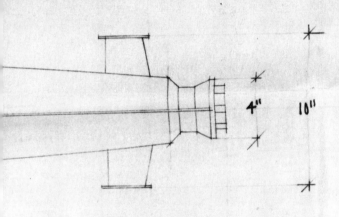

4"  10"

PLAN AND ELEVATIONS SHEWING DESIGN
AND CONSTRUCTION OF ROCKET SHIP. THE
SHIP IN THE MODEL WILL LOOK AS IF
CRASHED AND IS TO BE BUILT NOT AS ABOVE
BUT AS SHEWN ON SHEET '2'
MODEL IS TO HAVE AS MUCH SMALL DETAIL
AS POSSIBLE FOR CLOSE UP SHOTS.
FINISH IN SILVER WITH SOME METALIC
GREY PARTS, BLACK AND WHITE CHECKS ON
SIDES, LETTERING IN RED.

SEVERAL TYPES OF SHOTS WILL BE REQUIRED
OF THE MODEL. THE FIRST ESTABLISHING (LONG)
SHOT WILL BE HIGH ANGLE AS SHEWN
ON ENCLOSED DIAGRAM, REMAINING SHOTS
WILL BE CLOSE-UPS.

STOCK

**BBC tv**  DESIGN DEPARTMENT

| SHEET NO. 1 | DATE DRAWN 22/10/64 |
| NO. OF SHEETS | SCALE |

DISTRIBUTION

| ALLOCATIONS | DESIGNER EALING | ☑ PRODUCER |
| A.P.M. (TEL) | DESIGN ORGANISER | ☑ SCENE MASTER |
| BACK PROJECTION | DRAPES | ☑ ASST. SCENEMASTER |
| GRAPHICS | ELECTRICIANS | SCENERY STORES |
| CARPENTERS | ESTIMATOR | S·ENIC ARTISTS |
| CON. MANAGER | F.M's OFFICE | SPECIAL EFFECTS |
| DESIGNER | METAL WORKERS | SUPPLY FOREMAN |
| DESIGN ASST. | PAINTERS | SUPPLY ORGANISER |
| | (15) | ☑ OUTSIDE CONTRACT |

| ESTIMATOR | PRODUCER CHRIS BARRY |
| | DESIGNER RAYMOND CUSICK EXT 2436 |
| | DRAWN BY CHRIS THOMPSON |
| DATE 23-10-64 | ZERO DATE 4/11/64  V.T.R. DATE |
| A.D.O. | FILM DATE 4-20/11/64 TRANS. DATE |
| | PRODUCTION |
| DATE 23/10/64 | DR WHO (TV) |
| STUDIO 3A·3B. | 236B  PRODUCTION NUMBER |

In the event Spooner found he had little to do in setting up most of Season Two's stories. Thorough as ever, Whitaker had already commissioned and worked on scripts by Bill Strutton and Glyn Jones, and penned one himself about the Crusades. Spooner's own Roman Empire story was in the pipeline, leaving only an initial vacancy for a story to replace Carole Ann Ford's character. And Whitaker filled that vacuum as well . . .

Another two part 'quickie', 'The Rescue' was put together fairly cheaply to introduce the new teenage lead played by Maureen O'Brien. The Production Office laboured at some length to find the right name for the character. David Whitaker originally chose Milly, a name dropped due to its close public association with a young Jamaican pop singer of the time. Then, for a while the character was named Tanni, before it finally got changed, on Spooner's rewrite, to Vicki.

Sets left over from the space ship in 'The Sensorites' were re-used for the interiors of crashed British Rocket Ship 201, while Tristram Cary's *musique concrète* from 'The Daleks' got its second airing as well.

Aside from two unspeaking extras and a voice-over artist, the only addition to the cast was actor Ray Barrett, playing both Bennett and Koquillion. To disguise the revelation that Bennett was Koquillion, Verity Lambert, supplying the cast details for Episode One to *Radio Times*, listed Koquillion as being played by Sydney Wilson. A pseudonym, Sydney Wilson was a combination of the names of Verity Lambert's two immediate department heads . . .

PREVIOUS PAGE:
The UK201 rocket on Dido, where the TARDIS crew met Vicki. Sets from 'The Sensorites' were reused for the interior of the rocket.

BELOW:
The crashed UK201 rocket on the planet Dido, as seen on screen.

## Production Credits

Serial 'L'
Two Episodes
Black and White

| | |
|---|---|
| 'The Powerful Enemy' | 2 January 1965 |
| 'Desperate Measures' | 9 January 1965 |

### Cast

| | |
|---|---|
| Doctor Who | William Hartnell |
| Ian Chesterton | William Russell |
| Barbara Wright | Jacqueline Hill |
| Vicki | Maureen O'Brien |
| | |
| Bennett | Ray Barrett |
| Space captain/sand | Tom Sheridan |
| monster | Sydney Wilson |
| Koquillion | John Stuart, Colin Hughes |
| Didonians | |

### Crew

| | |
|---|---|
| Production Assistant | David Maloney |
| Assistant Floor Manager | Valerie Wilkins |
| Costume Supervisor | Daphne Dare |
| Make-up Supervisor | Sonia Markham |
| Incidental Music | Tristram Cary |
| Story Editor | Dennis Spooner |
| Designer | Raymond P. Cusick |
| Associate Producer | Mervyn Pinfield |
| Producer | Verity Lambert |
| Director | Christopher Barry |

# THE WAR MACHINES

IT BEGAN with a script. Initially Terry Nation declined to work on *Doctor Who* when the invitation came through, being far too busy at the time writing for Tony Hancock on tour in Nottingham. It was Nation's close friend Dennis Spooner who had put his name forward to David Whitaker, showing him the science fiction script Nation had done for Irene Shubik's *Out of this World* series a year or so earlier.

However, as the now-famous story purports, the evening after Nation had instructed his agent to say no to the *Doctor Who* offer, he and Tony Hancock had a serious disagreement, resulting in the writer catching the first train back to London the following morning, with no work, and a central heating system in his flat to pay for. Nation anxiously telephoned his agent to ask if she had formally rejected the *Doctor Who* offer. As luck would have it the letter had not been sent. So, straight away, Terry Nation sat down at his typewriter and began work on the first phase of any TV writing project, the story idea.

Terry Nation read the Whitaker/Webber Writer's Guide for

Ray Cusick and his diabolical creations. As a BBC employee, Cusick received little financial return for creating one of the most memorable monsters of all time.

*Doctor Who* and noted the paragraph about sf stories using a
known scientific premise as their basis. Something of a keen
student of modern history Nation had two main preoccupations –
technological warfare and the ideals of the European dictatorships
in the Thirties and Forties. In particular Nation had long held a
morbid fascination with the horrors of contemporary warfare: gas
attack, chemical shelling and especially with the effects of nuclear
weapons. Recently he had been intrigued by a paper proposing the
development of an atomic weapon designed to kill people through
massive exposure to radioactive fallout, but with a limited blast
capability, thereby keeping buildings relatively intact – the
Neutron Bomb.

He decided to base his *Doctor Who* story around a world where
this nuclear nightmare had already happened. The heat flash of an
enormously powerful neutron bomb had carbonised a planet with
the ensuing radioactive fallout condemning its survivors to the full
horrors of atrophy and mutation.

For one race Nation envisaged mutation running full circle,
evolving the species into tall, elegant, blond haired superfolk – the
epitomy of the Aryan ideal. These were the Thals. The other
species, more technologically adept, sought sanctuary for their
decaying bodies by encasing them in survival suits. These were the
Daleks, creatures devoid of sentiment and emotion, their minds as
scarred with bitterness as their bodies were scarred with decay.
Appropriately, Nation named his world Skaro.

David Whitaker loved the storyline, rapidly commissioned the
episode-by-episode story breakdown, and as quickly commissioned
the full scripts. His work done, Nation collected his fee and
promptly set off in search of other work, as did any other jobbing
writer.

With the scripts turned over to Christopher Barry and Raymond
Cusick some of the earliest discussions centred around the form
and shape of these Dalek survivors. More noted for his skills with
dialogue, Nation's description of the survival-suited aliens ran to
just one paragraph. It said:

'Hideous machine-like creatures, they are legless, moving on a
round base. They have no human features. A lens on a flexible
shaft acts as an eye. Arms with mechanical grips for hands.'

It was the kind of loose description a teacher might hand out to
a class of pupils and ask for drawings based on its inspiration. All
the resulting drawings would, odds on, be completely different
from one another. So for the BBC-designed Dalek the
all-important inspiration could only really come from one source;
Raymond Cusick.

'The idea for the Dalek came from my mind. I knew initially I
didn't want a man in a silver suit with a mask over his head – the
sort of thing you see in fairgrounds. I just didn't feel the Dalek
was like that. From the script it tells you that after this nuclear war
the creatures are supposed to have decayed into these horrible
shapes, almost armless and legless, dependent on machines to give
them any mobility. So I decided, right from the beginning, there
should be nothing to suggest walking.

120

Taking the lid off the Daleks. Note the black background above the lift: a help to the inlay operator whose equipment will give the illusion of the lift moving.

'I telephoned Terry Nation, asking what he felt about them. All he said was, "Did you see the Georgian State Dancers?" I said yes. He said, "Remember the peasant dance where they came out in the long, hooped skirts and you can't see their feet? That's what I'm aiming at, a gliding motion where you can't see any legs."'

'So obviously I was thinking along the same lines as him. The pepper pot idea first came about one lunchtime while I was having lunch with Chris Barry and Mervyn Pinfield. Having already told them how I proposed they should move I demonstrated it by moving one of the pepper pots around the table.

'Mervyn had suggested we should make the Dalek transport machines out of cardboard tubes – sprayed silver and fitted over a person's legs. I said to Chris I felt we had a bit more money and could do better than that. So it was then a question of just sitting down with a blank sheet of paper and starting to draw, because a Designer thinks about structures and design only by doing it, by drawing what's in his mind.

'So I thought, well there's got to be an operator inside, so it has to be based around a person. I didn't want the person standing up because then you were back to the body shape, so he had to be sitting down. I drew a chair which was ergonomically eighteen inches from the ground and sketched an average sized person sitting on it. That idea I soon modified to incorporate a smaller actor, thinking it would be better if we lost the human size similarity altogether.

'Once you've got that basic drawing of a person sitting sideways on a chair, if you draw straight lines around him you've more or less got a pyramid shape. So the silhouette of the Dalek actually came directly from the shape of a person sitting down in a chair.

121

'Next it was important that the operator should be able to see out all around him but without the viewers seeing there was someone obviously inside. So there had to be a slit or something. I thought of the metal gauze idea because when light hits a gauze cylinder you can't see behind it although anyone inside can look out, and when you put the louvres across as well you further disguise their presence.

'The next point I had to work out logically was how the operator would get inside. It had to have a break in it somewhere, but it too shouldn't be obvious from the outside.

'Similarly, I didn't want any obvious arms on it so I had to work out a system of manipulators – things that did things, like a grip mechanism or a gun. There was no point having an arm with a gun attached to it, so I decided just to have the gun itself, rather like a tank.'

The pepper pot analogy kept coming back to Raymond Cusick as he began sketching his ideas down onto paper. One of the very first sketches took the salt cellar shape literally with the design of the skirt section mirroring the corrugations on the pot, and the eye/gun turret ressembling the screw-off lid. Cusick quickly rejected this design, possibly for its obvious associations, and definitely because of limitations with the manipulators. This initial drawing saw the arms being worked from wires, marionette style, by another operator on a gantry. Fine for a static Dalek, but totally inappropriate for a mobile machine.

Cusick's second design saw the Dalek closer to its final form. This version was more conical, losing its basic smoothness only at the head section above the louvres, where sat the eye and sensor apparatus fixed on a rotating turret.

The arm mounting, fitted to the body at operator neck height by a rubber joint, contained an extendable piston rod with a pair of jaw grips at the end which could be flexed by the actor inside. Directly below this arm, also emerging from one of the circular indents on the midriff, was the gun, suggesting each circle was a panel behind which lay other implements the Dalek might use if required.

Unhappy with this design as well, which he felt looked ungainly and awkward, Cusick tried again with a wider based shape, this time moving the studded circles down from the midriff to the skirt section.

'One of my early thoughts was to have the base unit moulded with two skins. The outer skin would be moulded in clear perspex or similar with an inner skin behind it. The latter would be about three of four inches away from the outer, transparent skin and its surface would be mirrored or coated in some reflective material. In the gap I was planning to have a whole lot of lights and electronic valves which could light up and flash when the Dalek was agitated about anything. It would, I hoped, create the illusion that you could see through the base, dispelling any impression there was an operator inside.'

Cost ruled out adopting this idea, which might have presented problems as Cusick tackled how to steer and motivate the casing.

ABOVE:
Cusick's first drawing for the Dalek machine, based on a pepper pot, with arms on remotely operated wires

BELOW:
A later design, featuring the more familiar louvred slats, the rotating eye turret, the centrally mounted arm, and the hemisphere panels.

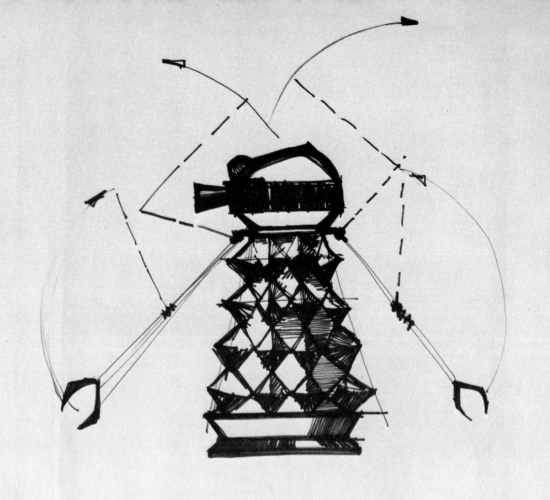

5'10"

castors

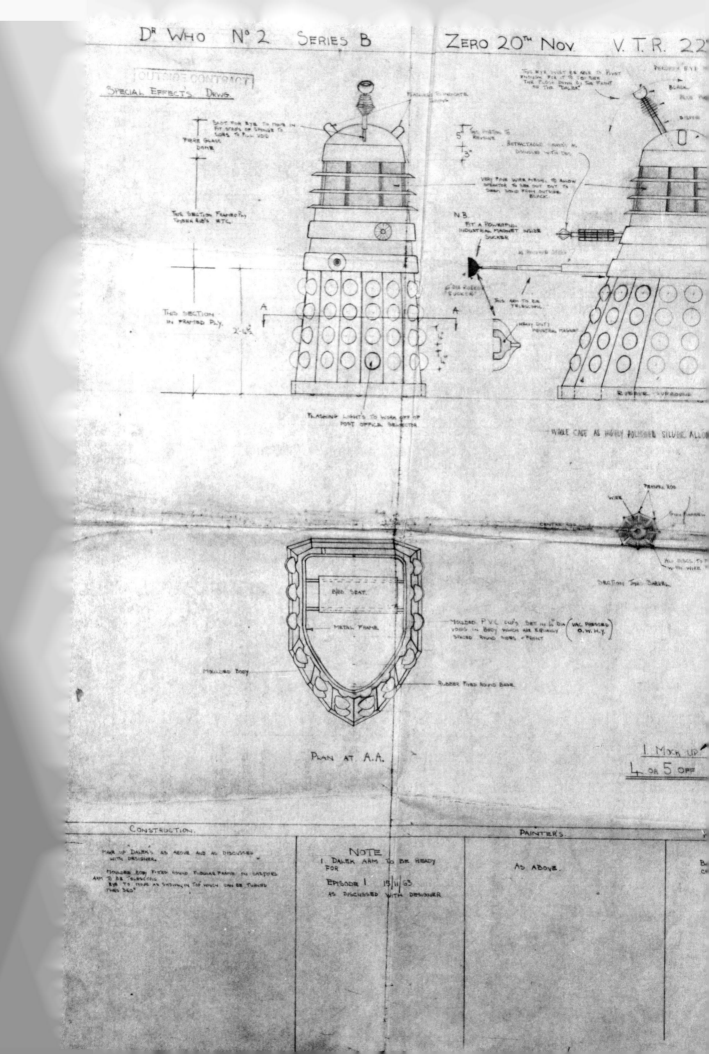

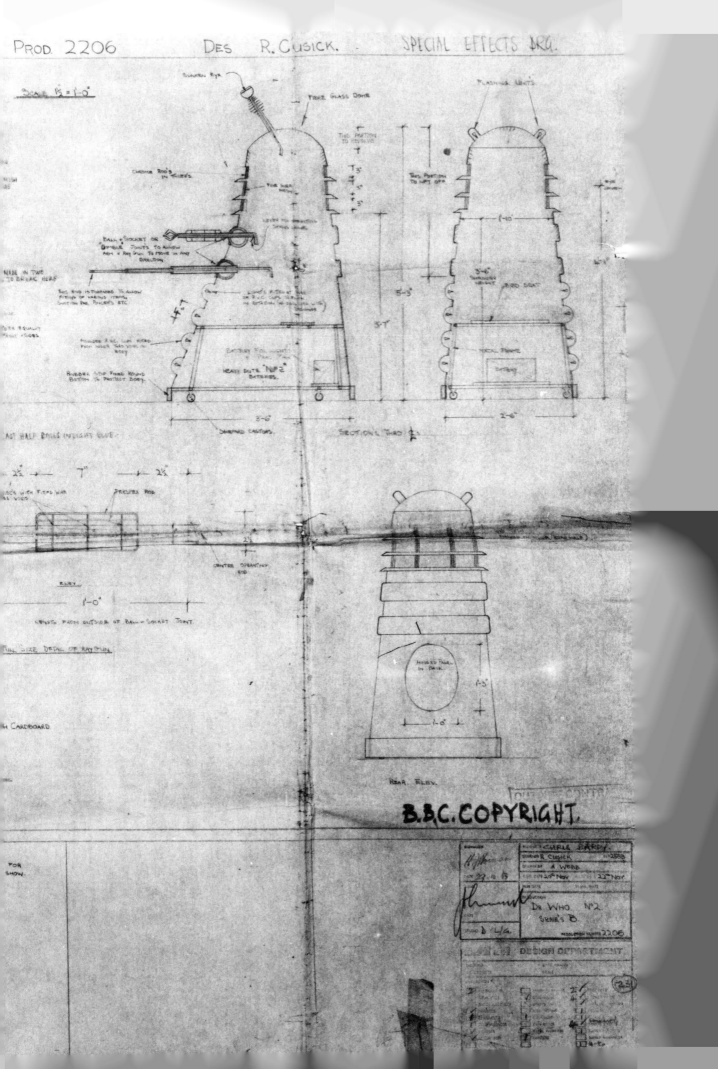

The eventual colour illustration, put before Verity Lambert and Christopher Barry at the Monday meeting, proved very close to the design finally adopted. At this stage the hand and gun mechanisms were still on a vertical, rather than horizontal, plane, but in most other respects it was *the* Dalek.

At this stage the Dalek casing housed a children's tricycle, seated on which the operator could steer and pedal his machine.

Never having designed anything like this before Cusick privately held many worries about the cost and ease of manufacturing these props. With little experience of Visual Effects construction techniques, Cusick was concerned lest the labour fees involved (the costliest part of any Effects job) would make his drawings cost-impractical. The original plan to make the skirt section conical was a victim of this thinking, although totally by accident rather than design . . .

'I felt I needed advice about the base unit because I wasn't sure how easy it would be to mass produce from the prototype which had hemispheres studded into it. So I showed my drawing to one of the Visual Effects Designers. He immediately told me that to do a smoothly coned skirt would be vastly expensive in terms of bending and shaping wood, and equally expensive to do as the multi-part mould which he reckoned was necessary because of the protruding hemispheres.

'So I compromised by redesigning the base as a set of flat plates with circular holes cut in them through which sets of moulded hemispheres could be pushed. That was the design I finally gave to *Shawcraft* as a construction drawing which ended up as the Dalek. Only after they were built did the Manager of *Shawcraft* ask me why I hadn't made the base more cone-shaped. I told them the arguments put forward by Visual Effects, only to be told in return manufacturing a conical base would have been much easier as it could all have been done from one two-part mould in half the time.'

The Daleks were built by *Shawcraft Models*, a freelance company of prop builders founded in 1947 by its present Manager Bill Roberts. In 1963, as now, the BBC did little in the way of in-house prop building due to the time and resources required for these highly specialised operations. *Shawcraft* had made its name as manufacturers of highly detailed architectural models – anything from miniatures of oil refineries to the large fibre-glass aircraft models common to many Travel Agents' windows.

The BBC found *Shawcraft* exceptionally efficient in building any form of electrical or mechanical special prop. The TARDIS console was their first job for *Doctor Who*, and thereafter a succession of their 'flashing light/moving part' props appeared in many serials, 'The Daleks', 'The Keys of Marinus', 'The Space Museum' and 'Galaxy Four' to name but a few.

Between them, Raymond Cusick and Bill Roberts worked out the practicalities of making the Dalek. An early casualty was the tricycle idea. Despite visits to dozens of toy shops, all they could find were tricycles that were either too large or too small for their requirements. The seat, therefore, would have to be part of the

PREVIOUS PAGE:
Almost the final blueprint for the Dalek. Note, however, that the gun and sucker are still on two different horizontal levels.

126

internal frame, steering would have to be manually done by the operator's feet pushing along the floor, and the hoped-for gliding motion achieved solely through sets of little castors hidden under the fender base.

On the manufacturing side the Dalek started life as a chalk line drawn on the factory floor around the portly frame of Bill Roberts seated on a stool. The prototype came first, built mostly from wood with modifications agreed between Roberts and Cusick as obstacles were encountered.

The biggest change was the midriff section. Although the skirt panels look perfectly flat when seen on air, in reality they follow varying angles to the original base vertical planes, bending ever so slightly as they rise up from the fender section to join up at the midriff. Cusick's original construction drawing had the midriff too narrow to allow the skirt flats to meet smoothly and so the midriff was widened. This in turn led to the arm and gun junction boxes being redesigned horizontally next to each other rather than grouped centrally at the front.

Thin strips of aluminium, bolted onto the midriff, successfully disguised the break in the casing that would allow the Operators to get in and out of their Dalek machines.

Ball and socket mechanisms replaced the original idea of rubber joints for the arm and gun due to hefty costs involved in manufacturing the latter. And, as a further saving, the notion of a mechanical grip for a hand was reluctantly abandoned in favour of the now infamous sink plunger.

Raymond Cusick had hoped for six Daleks from his budget but in the end the money only ran to affording four. Each Dalek weighed almost a hundredweight, stood 4′ 8″ high and cost £120. In an era when the average gross weekly wage was about £10 this made them very expensive props indeed.

The Daleks proved an immediate hit with the production cast and crew as they were delivered to Lime Grove's car park in time for the dress rehearsals. But it was only when these first rehearsals began that two more problems reared their heads.

Working together, Sound Supervisor Ray Angel and Radiophonic Workshop artist Brian Hodgson had devised a special voice for the Daleks. Trying out various ideas they eventually settled on the use of a Ring Modulator, which sets up a low frequency hum breaking up speech patterns into juddery, intermittent tones. Hodgson had already used this trick for a radio play, *Sword from the Stars*, to give a robot named Jones a haughty but very mechanical voice. This evolved into the unforgettable Dalek grating once voice artists Peter Hawkins and David Graham agreed to deliver their lines in very flat tones, clipping the consonants and lengthening the vowels. Ray Angel put the final touches, adding echo and reverberation when the voices were relayed down to the studio floor.

The problem Christopher Barry and Raymond Cusick quickly identified was that nobody could easily detect which Dalek was speaking. Furthermore, as each Dalek was physically identical, coaching each one in his directions was a nightmare.

The answer to problem one was a makeshift modification which ultimately added even more to the Dalek's appeal. Working against time Cusick had two holes drilled into each Dalek's dome section. He then wired through each hole a Christmas tree light bulb connected to a battery and a bell-push button. Lastly, a ping-pong ball fitted over each light bulb managed to disguise their Yuletide origins. Thus, if each operator learned his lines he could push the button inside his casing to make the lights flash on and off in synchronisation with the soundtrack.

Problem two, choreographing the Daleks, was solved by sticking numbered cards onto each Dalek during rehearsals, and by tacking different coloured sellotape marks onto the floor; colour red denoting Dalek Two for instance. Ironically this Heath Robinson make-do also ended up contributing to the Dalek myth. Having sellotaped the coloured strips onto the floor the sellotape reels were left sandwiched behind each Dalek's waistband as a further rehearsal aid – a red reel in Dalek Two's waistband for instance. Photographs taken during rehearsals (photographers are not allowed to take shots during live takes) showed up these sellotape reels clearly. Consequently when commercial artists and manufacturers

128

began using these photographs as reference for comic strips, book illustrations, box tops etc. they assumed the reel to be a speaker grill. Even to this day illustrations turn up showing Daleks with loudspeaker meshes mounted between their arm and gun rods, whereas in truth no television Dalek has ever sported such a contraption.

The aftermath of the Daleks' debut in *Doctor Who* has become history. Since that day many Designers, both amateur and professional, have turned their hands to making or modifying Daleks. Spencer Chapman, designing for 'The Dalek Invasion of Earth', managed to bring back the tricycle idea for getting the Daleks to move on rough terrain. But doing this required mounting each Dalek onto a specially enlarged fender frame to hide the pneumatic-tyred tricycle underneath.

In 1966, when the Visual Effects Department finally took on *Doctor Who*, they too rebuilt the Daleks, enlarging the midriff sections to make them wider and taller after operators had complained of chaffed and scraped shoulders.

Cusick himself remained the unsung creator of the Daleks for many years, picking up little recognition for his work. But one possession did come his way in 1965 of which he is very proud:

'We (the Design Department) got asked by the Producer of *Blue Peter* to come up with a full-size Dalek that children could build easily at home for about 10/6d. Eventually, after canvassing ideas from virtually everyone in the department, I came up with a design, using egg boxes and colanders which *Blue Peter* decided to use.

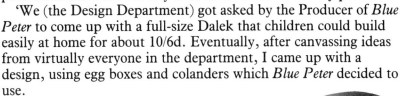

'They broadcast the show and at the end of it Christopher Trace [one of the presenters] said something like, "Whoever designed the Daleks really deserves a gold *Blue Peter* badge", which is the badge they only award for very, very special achievements.

'A week or so afterwards, not having heard any feedback from them, I rang the *Blue Peter* office to ask how it had gone, and I concluded by asking, only semi-seriously, what happened to my gold *Blue Peter* badge that Christopher Trace mentioned. A couple of days later, and to my amazement, one arrived in the post. I've still got it . . .'

130

# THE CELESTIAL TOYMAKER

'A DESIGNER is part of the creative team. His responsibility is the picture – what goes on screen, what appears in front of the screen. Not the actual shots, those the Director decides and works out for the style they're going to shoot in. But what they want to see – the physical image – that's where the Designer's expertise comes in.

'It isn't a question of the Designer working it out for the Director. It isn't a question of the Director working it out for the Designer. It's a shared responsibility between them to create the right environment so that the magic can happen.'

The term Designer, when applied to the visual medium, is almost as old as the medium itself. However, strange though it may seem, whenever criticism, favourable or unfavourable, is levelled at any sort of production, very rarely does the Designer's effort get a mention. Writers are credited with the inspiration, Directors, especially in the case of the film industry, are feted for the execution. Yet none of them in the triple realms of Theatre, Television and Film would be anywhere without the Designer.

A Designer creates the world that the Writer's mind will

populate and the Director's skills will orchestrate. His is the art of picture composition, and, such, his efforts are as invaluable to a production as that of his two other creative peers.

Raymond Cusick, along with fellow Senior Designer Barry Newbery, created the mood, the look and the environment of the early *Doctor Who* adventures. Their ingenuity with sets, their ideas on lighting, their careful arrangement of props, all established the intangible, but very distinct, atmosphere and mood of the Hartnell serials. Particularly during the first two seasons when, between them, they worked virtually non-stop on the programme, they established a continuity of ideas and standards that worked very well, helping to settle in sceptical and dubious new viewers to the series.

Cusick even goes so far as to venture an empathy between the teams Verity Lambert assembled to work on the series.

'When you worked with Directors like Christopher Barry or Douglas Camfield, initially you'd spend endless time in discussions, working out the best way to shoot a script. But after a few shows together you got to the point where you could read each other's thoughts. I knew what they had in mind, they knew my way of working, which cut down enormously on the number of meetings we needed to plan shows out.

'Good Directors use the Designer as an adviser. They have vague ideas of the type of pictures they're looking for, so they're trying to get the Designer to make it happen for them – to confirm their thoughts.'

The disciplines a Designer works by demand some very special qualities – in effect they demand a specialist in many wide-ranging fields, coupled with virtual Sherlock Holmes powers of observation.

'Generally Designers start by going to Art School where they begin doing Basic Design before, later, they specialise in some form of three dimensional design. You can divide Art into two groups: two-dimensional which is flat – painting, sketching, illustration – and three-dimensional which encompasses space and volume. A lot of Television Designers trained as architects, some as Exhibition and Interior Designers. I trained as a Theatre Designer, but all three are about space and volume with people in it.

'As for the flair, that's not something you can acquire. You've either got it or you haven't. It's like saying why is somebody a better pianist than his colleague, even though they both went to the same conservatory. It's intuitive. It has to be. You also need to have an interest in the business of Television to enable you to understand a Director's requirements. You must like stories, you must like seeing films yourself.

'A Designer in Television must have a very wide general knowledge. Preferably they should have a strong literary interest; an interest in reading stories. A lot of them like photography, many others have a fascination with architecture, and how people use architecture in terms both of the past, including costumes and social history, and with the present. Above all else, a Designer must be watching all the time, watching everything . . .'

132

Nowhere is the art of the Designer needed more than when a script calls for an entirely new world to be created, as was so often the case in *Doctor Who*.

Because of the show's alternation between historical tales and science fiction adventures, it happened that Barry Newbery wound up doing most of the stories in Earth's past, while Raymond Cusick got the bulk of the sf material – an on-going process that tested his imagination to the limits.

'Terry Nation often used to describe a set as a plain, white room. So when I met him once I asked him "Why do you do that?"; to which he replied, "I couldn't think of anything else. It's up to you. Do what you like". So then it was up to me to go back to the script and find what I could to give me a lead.

'If you have a room which is meant to be a meeting place of all the chief Daleks, and what they're talking about is power – power over other civilisations, power over other planets – then power and domination is what comes through in the dialogue, and is the feeling behind what you want to create. So then you start thinking about visual images which give you this impression of power and menace, something like the Nuremberg Rallies of the 1930s, and use that as the basis of your inspiration. Ideally you might like to end up with a set which, even if only subconsciously, reminds you of the atmosphere and tension of those rallies.'

Despite their hefty involvement with *Doctor Who* for over two years neither Raymond Cusick nor Barry Newbery designed the TARDIS. That task fell to Polish-born Designer Peter Brachaki.

The interior design of the TARDIS proved to be a text-book illustration of Cusick's rule-of-thumb about seeking impressions as a guide to inspiration.

In Coburn's original script, which became the pilot episode, operation of the ship was clearly the sole preserve of the Doctor. Therefore, reasoned Brachaki, a one-man operated craft would need all its controls close together and within easy reach of its solo pilot. On the basis of that modular thinking came the somewhat revolutionary idea (for 1963) of the single, ergonomically efficient control console.

Similarly the glass column – later titled the Time Rotor in a Terry Nation script – was originally conceived as a navigational aid of very advanced design. To human beings it might appear as a random jumble of instrumentation, but to those of the Doctor's civilisation one glance at its internal configuration would enable the pilot to work out his position in time and space. As built, the original Time Rotor could not only rise and fall but rotate on its axis as well.

The TARDIS walls, fashioned in a style that would nowadays be called 'hi-tech', were also revolutionary for their era and were deliberately styled to give a timeless look; something equally suited to ancient Egypt as to the distant future. His original intention was to have the walls constructed out of fibre glass, but costs proved prohibitive and so they were made from wood with vacuum-formed PVC roundels used for the indents. Even then, not all the walls were wood. One or two were photographic

133

blow-ups, mounted on plywood struts and battens, inspired from a three-inch square sheet of plastic Brachaki had in his possession while he was contemplating the design.

To suggest the hidden but omnipresent power of the TARDIS Brachaki wanted a system of lights behind the roundels that would make them glow and pulse while the ship was in flight. This too had to be curbed on cost grounds, along with plans for two monolithic block-like structures, within the control room, which would darken to black as the ship landed, and fill with light as it took off. Then, as now, the materials just were not available to make that a feasible proposition.

For the original pilot episode the TARDIS interior set covered a full half of Studio D's floor space. But even here the Designer had carefully thought out its use in subsequent stories when, perhaps, the ship would not play so vital a role. All the TARDIS sections were integrated, like a jigsaw, and could be arranged in any number of abstract ways without the visual suggestion of the set being lost. Once the full-size version had been seen and digested by the viewer, it was only then necessary to include the doors, the console and one or two wall sections for the illusion to be maintained.

Peter Brachaki designed all the sets for the pilot episodes, but for health reasons was unavailable for the remount, and subsequently for the year-round production schedule. By then Verity Lambert had established her notion of production teams and the Design jobs were allocated out to Barry Newbery and Raymond Cusick.

For Cusick, who had joined the BBC as a Design Assistant in 1960 and become a Designer proper in 1962, his move into *Doctor Who* was almost accidental. The original Designer scheduled for 'The Daleks' was Ridley Scott – the same Ridley Scott who, years later, would win world renown for feature films like 'Alien' and 'Blade Runner'. Scott initially accepted the brief before discovering, due to other programme commitments, that he would not be free to handle design of the film sequences over at Ealing Studios. A quick reshuffle followed, and Cusick was brought in at short notice.

Straight away, however, one major problem area presented itself. The BBC's own internal Visual Effects Department, run by its devisor Jack Kine, was, in 1963, still a comparatively small affair, although fighting hard to win increased resources and cash to cope with the rising tide of effects requirements. So far Kine had had little success persuading the BBC's higher management to take his Department more seriously, so when *Doctor Who* came along he saw a golden opportunity.

Being also part of the 'old guard' who had been somewhat resentful of Sydney Newman's wind of change, Kine issued a flat 'No' when he was asked, by Mervyn Pinfield, to take on the enormous effects requirements of *Doctor Who*'s science fiction stories. To the astute Kine, such a refusal would have one of two results, both beneficial to Visual Effects in the long run. Either he would lose *Doctor Who*, in which case his small Department would save themselves a very large overhead, or the BBC would let go its purse strings a little and permit Kine to take on more staff and resources to handle such a project.

After some wrangling, option one prevailed and Visual Effects lost *Doctor Who* – at least for the time being . . . For Verity Lambert and Mervyn Pinfield, though, they still had the headache of scripts littered with special props and effects, and no-one to handle them.

Thus it transpired, for the only time in the BBC's history, that the Design Department was asked to undertake the responsibility and the budgets for all visual effects, special props, models, etc., needed for the television series.

As such a unique exercise it had its rewards and its penalties. It gave Raymond Cusick a far greater guarantee of artistic control over the series. He could plan miniature sets, devise intricate special props and know they would blend in perfect harmony with the sets he was designing. And it would give *Doctor Who* a far greater visual continuity as there would be no need to worry about give-and-take discussions with formal Effects Designers.

The penalties, though, were pressures of time and deadlines, coupled with trepidation about handling the area of Effects which was so totally outside Design's normal field of endeavour.

'All the stories, for which scripts were available, seemed very interesting, different, expensive and potentially difficult to do – a challenge to our limited resources.

'We had a freelance company of exhibition and display prop builders on our books called *Shawcraft Models* of Uxbridge, whom I quickly contracted to make most of our effects. They had a good reputation for being able to develop mechanical ideas if you briefed them well (they had already built the TARDIS console for Peter Brachaki). But though they were excellent makers of models to other people's plans and designs I quickly found they could only work well if they were given very detailed constructional drawings and plans. It was absolutely no good just giving them a sketch and expecting them to expand on it using their own initiative. Everything had to be carefully mapped out for them.

'An example: the Dalek city I wanted to be a complex structure of low metal towers, ramps and spires, quite detailed, possibly with some kind of perimeter wall or fence surrounding it. I drew this up as a sketch showing, in essence, a section of the city. This I gave to *Shawcraft*. A week later I was invited to take a look at the finished model, discovering then to my horror they had reproduced my sketch to the letter. Everything I had drawn was there, but nothing more. And the result was painfully crude to look at.

'So from then on I had to make sure that everything I presented to *Shawcraft* was in the form of a very concise constructional drawing – and that took time – a lot of time.

'The second main problem was dividing what time you had between sets and effects. And so demanding was *Doctor Who* that both Barry and I were working sixty- and seventy-hour weeks in those days, consistently. To give you another example, the initial

design for the Dalek had to be prepared for a Monday morning meeting. The only time I had was five hours on the Sunday beforehand, and that was supposed to be a rest day.'

The Designer's involvement with a story begins, like that of the Director, with the script. Nothing less than a script will do because so many of the key visual elements will only be apparent through the dialogue. Very few writers, in Cusick's experience, do much in the way of scene setting, and so a lot has to come from reading the dialogue and forming impressions in the mind. A perennial problem on the early *Doctor Who* stories was the lack of a full set of scripts by the 'Director Joining Date', which is roughly the time the Designer gets involved as well. This was especially true of the first Dalek serial which had many rewrites done to it before it was finally handed to Christopher Barry and Raymond Cusick.

The rejected model of the Dalek city on Skaro. Although it had followed Cusick's design, the model was not judged to look busy enough. The hills and the backdrop were also rejected.

OVERLEAF:
The final accepted model of the Dalek city. The mountains in this version are based on the Alps. Twenty-foot square, the table-top model was shot on film at Ealing.

The theme of the story was that something very sinister had happened a long time ago which had left the planet looking entirely different from anywhere you could see on Earth. The Daleks themselves, when you saw them, were meant to be entirely different from human beings, with a city that was built without any regard for human concepts of scale, size and functioning. The city was designed for these machines even down to the shape of control switches on their instruments.

'As you read the story you found yourself punching up shots in your mind, and you got a strong set of pictures forming which you could then draw down.

'Metal, the metallic theme which ran throughout the city's design, was essential. The Daleks' power was conducted through the floors so you instantly dismissed any idea of the city being built from house bricks.

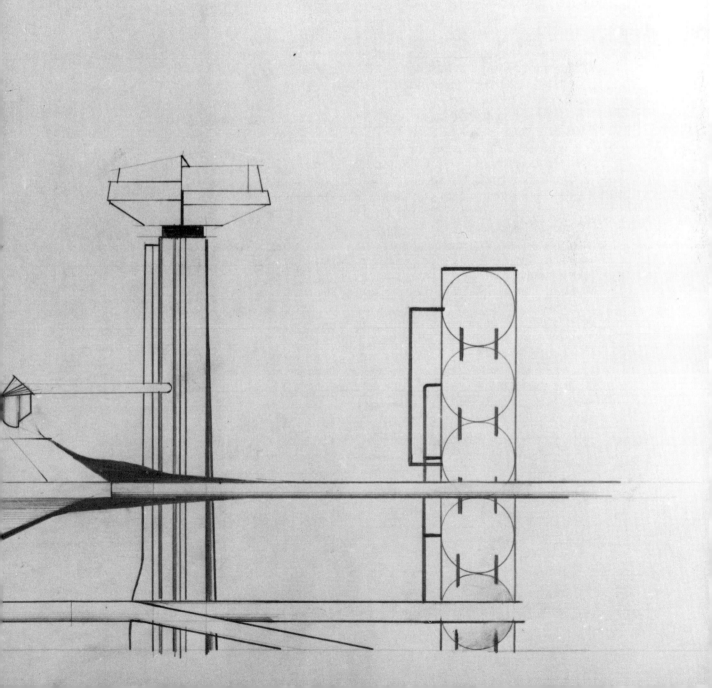

'Now all this basic planning does take time, which is why it is essential that we come onto a programme during its very early planning stages. All our work has to be prepared so much in advance, because then all the sets have to be constructed, all the statistics worked out, budgets have to be agreed and so on.

'If you are delayed, for whatever reason, from doing the above, then it causes a knock-on delay throughout the whole system. The Director, remember, starts with nothing. All he's got is a set of scripts, if he's lucky, some idea of who he wants in the cast, and perhaps a feel for how the show is going to be shot. It's up to you to give him the visual reference material from which he can start planning his camera angles, his cast positionings, etc.'

The limiting of television pictures to black and white only (colour did not arrive for BBC 1 until late 1969) was frustrating to Designers like Cusick, more inspired by the colour and splash of the Theatre. Although all sets and costumes were designed in colour, a lot of ingenuity needed to be applied to make the sets visually more interesting to the viewers; compensating them for only seeing everything in monochrome and through a slightly muzzy 405 line picture. A key element in disguising the physically small dimensions of most studios was lighting.

'Lighting can try and compensate for the lack of colour by creating certain moods. This was developed very highly in the Hollywood movies of the Thirties where they attempted to put "colour" into the pictures in terms of light and shade. It was very highly stylised, putting enormous shadows behind Errol Flynn and Basil Rathbone as they fenced up the steps of an equally stylised castle.

'With *Doctor Who*, as on any programme, it's very important to have discussions with the Technical Operations Manager about where lights should be positioned to create the mood you're after. Basically, any set is dead until light is thrown onto it.'

Backdrops is another key area farmed out to the Designer. Where location filming is not possible for exterior scenes, very often it will fall to the Designer to create realistic backdrops to maintain the illusion of a city or a forest stretching miles away into the distance.

Both 'The Daleks' and 'The Sensorites' featured very elaborate backdrops, all of which Cusick had first to draft out as large, highly detailed colour illustrations long before the day when the Scenic Artist would come in to paint them up.

Neither could these illustrations just be rough approximations of the finished articles. The perspectives, the horizon points, the viewing angles all had to be worked out beforehand so that camera shots would enable the backdrops to appear as natural continuations of the sets, instead of suddenly sloping up or downhill. If a crane camera was to be used, for instance, it would be no use designing a backdrop with a vanishing point relevant to one of its pedestal mounted brethren.

Once illustrated, each backdrop design had to be overlaid with a precise grid pattern as an aid for the scenic artist. The artist would reproduce that grid onto a studio canvas in a proportionately larger

PREVIOUS PAGE:
An architectural elevation depicting the hub of the Dalek city with its council chamber nerve centre.

144

scale, using it as a sequence of reference points by which to plot and paint up the landscape configuration exactly to the Design drawing.

Frequently, and particularly in the untried area of Effects, where everything is virtually a one-off enterprise, trial and experimentation prove the only way to solve apparently insoluble problems.

'One of the early Dalek episodes had a Thal going down to the shore of a lake at night to collect some water. He looks up, the script said, and sees above him the huge, luminous eyes of a monster.

'We knew, just by looking at it, there was no way we could do the scene exactly as it was written, so we compromised. I had made up a sort of flattened octopus-like creature, with electrically lit eyes, which we stretched out onto a frame and placed in a shallow trough of water so that it was only just submerged. Beneath the main body of the creature I placed a small, inflatable rubber ring, one of the type you buy at seasides, connected by a hose to an air pump. Finally we added dry ice to the trough to make the water bubble and to put a thin layer of mist over it.

'So what you ended up with was a shot of the Thal looking up, followed by a cut to a low angle close up of the trough where, by pumping up the rubber ring, the body of the monster was made to rise out of the water. With no other point of reference to its size, the impression given, by the establishing angle of the actor's gaze, was of something very large indeed surfacing. I was quite pleased with it.'

Not always, though, did effects shots proceed as smoothly. The script for 'The Chase', also by Terry Nation, called for Episode One to end with a Dalek rising dramatically out of the sand to menace the time-travellers. On this occasion the Director, against Cusick's advice, decided to do the shot by actually burying a full-size Dalek in a sand pit, the idea being to use a tow rope, attached to a Land Rover, to pull the machine from its sandy grave. The filming crew spent a full morning digging a suitably sized pit with a sloping ramp, filling it in again once the Dalek had been rolled into place. Only when the cameras were rolling was it heart-sinkingly apparent that the physics of inertia, represented by nearly a ton of resting sand, were greater than the physics of motion represented by the four skidding wheels of a Land Rover.

There was little mirth among the film crew, least of all from Raymond Cusick whose job it suddenly became to pull a last minute rabbit out of the hat. As things worked out the hat/rabbit analogy was nearer the truth than anyone suspected. As the recording deadline approached *Shawcraft*, under Cusick's guidance, fashioned a one-fifth scale model Dalek with remotely operated limbs and turret dome. Sunk into a table top model of the sand pit a simple push from below achieved in seconds what a location shoot failed to do in a day.

Not always were Cusick's warnings ignored by Directors, as in the case of working on Episode One of 'The Keys of Marinus' with John Gorrie.

'If you remember the scene, a Voord is fighting with Ian when he gets thrown back against a wall. A trap door in the wall then swings open and the Voord tumbles through to perish in a pool of acid hundreds of feet below the centre of the pyramid. I asked John how he planned to do this shot and he said, "Simple. We just have a sliding door in the wall, operated by one of the scenic crew. The door opens, the Voord falls through, the door shuts again."

'I told him there and then that shot wouldn't work. The viewers would just assume he'd fallen into a cupboard and bang would go the impact of the scene. It's a cardinal rule Designers work to that you never upset the audience by breaking the train of suspense. John agreed this, which is why we finished up with a little model set showing the chimney behind the wall, down which a miniature Voord could be thrown.'

'The Keys of Marinus' is the one story for *Doctor Who* Cusick looks back on with a shudder. The script's call for virtually six new sets *every week* evolved into an unrelenting treadmill of pure trauma.

'Nothing worked on that one. Everything went wrong. It was a hell of a job even to complete some episodes when the money ran out. There were whole sequences of effects – rotating stone idols, descending ceilings with protruding spikes, moving plant vines – whole sequences which, on a feature film, would cost a lot to set up, and take weeks, possibly months, to film. And we were trying to do it all in one day, just twelve hours . . .

'Even on the most ordinary of programmes the amount of work you do on sets as they come into the studio – preparing them, repairing them even, making them shootable – is quite involved. So when you have sets with collapsing walls, ceilings of spikes, etc., all required to work in a live environment, it's tantamount to doing a live stage production really. But at least on a stage production you'll have rehearsed it all. You'll have spent at least one day testing everything to see if it's okay before you show it to the public. We didn't have that. We didn't even have a couple of hours.

'The demands, in a sense, were ridiculous for Television as it was in that time. But we did it . . . though I wouldn't want to do it again.'

Considerably more rewarding were some of the elaborate effects tried out for 'Planet of Giants', worked out in collusion with Producer Mervyn Pinfield and trainee Director Douglas Camfield.

'We used a half-silvered mirror to achieve a very tricky shot indeed. A giant had just been shot. He's lying on the ground, and one of the inch-high companions walks in front of his face to verify he's dead. We worked out there were several ways we could compose a visual picture, before we settled on using the mirror technique.

'Placing a half-silvered mirror in front of a camera allowed the camera to see two images simultaneously, providing you'd balanced out lighting the two images very carefully. The mirror

146

Cusick's model for the studio design of Ancient Rome.

was mounted midway between the camera and a 4′ × 3′ caption slide of the dead man's face and tilted to a 45° angle. To the left of the camera, and probably at the other end of the studio to get the size ratio right, we had a black draped set for the miniaturised companion to walk in front of. So the cameraman, looking through his viewfinder, could see the caption slide through the glass plate, plus sufficient reflection of the action going on over at the black drape set. Lighting then became critical to ensure you didn't swamp one image with the other.'

'Planet of Giants' was the penultimate story of the first season production-wise, but for regular members of the production team there was little, if any, time for resting. Within weeks of finishing the 'Giants' serial, Cusick was hard at work again, designing no less than two stories back-to-back: 'The Rescue' and his first historical serial 'The Romans', which presented something of a challenge:

'Designing Ancient Rome was in fact more difficult than the science fiction adventures, because one was recreating somewhere that actually existed, and you had to be as accurate as you could within the limits of the budget. The fire effects were awful, very embarrassing, and due entirely to a lack of money.'

The decision to continue *Doctor Who* for a second year-round season brought matters to a head between the Production Office and its two Designers. 'The workload for both Barry Newbery

147

and myself was tremendous, we both felt we could not go on much longer, and suggested that a third Designer be included on the team.'

John Wood (who later left the BBC to work on feature films) was the first, cutting his teeth on the grandiose and very expensive 'The Web Planet' serial, with Spencer Chapman second on 'The Space Museum'. Chapman had already done one *Doctor Who*, 'The Dalek Invasion of Earth', brought in at short notice due to Cusick's commitments on the 'Planet of Giants' story.

The appointment of fresh Designers to the series finally broke the ping-pong philosophy that had so threatened to trap Newbery and Cusick forever on the *Doctor Who* treadmill. They completed the epic length 'The Daleks' Master Plan' story as a joint endeavour early in 1966, but thereafter they expressed a wish to branch outwards and explore new design horizons. Newbery felt quite happy about returning to the series on a very irregular basis, but for Cusick enough was enough.

'I had worked on *Doctor Who* since the middle of 1963, the work involved had been very hard and I felt exhausted. I felt I needed different challenges, to move on. *Doctor Who*, especially nowadays, is the type of programme they put fairly new Designers on to test their abilities. For me it was a welcome challenge at the time and, in retrospect, I enjoyed it. I am a Drama man. I started off that way in the Theatre, but like most, you have (by force of necessity) to be able to turn your hand to whatever is needed of you.

'Do I pride myself on being one element in the show's overall success? I often have wondered what the Dalek might have been if some other Designer had designed it. Ridley Scott's design might have been very interesting because he was, and is, an excellent Designer. Yes, I suppose I do feel proud of my efforts to help *Doctor Who*'s production.'

ABOVE:
The Senate antechamber from 'The Romans', populated by a host of stock Roman columns.

BELOW:
More stock columns for this banqueting room from 'The Romans'. Also featured were wall dividers which had previously been seen in 'The Keys of Marinus'.

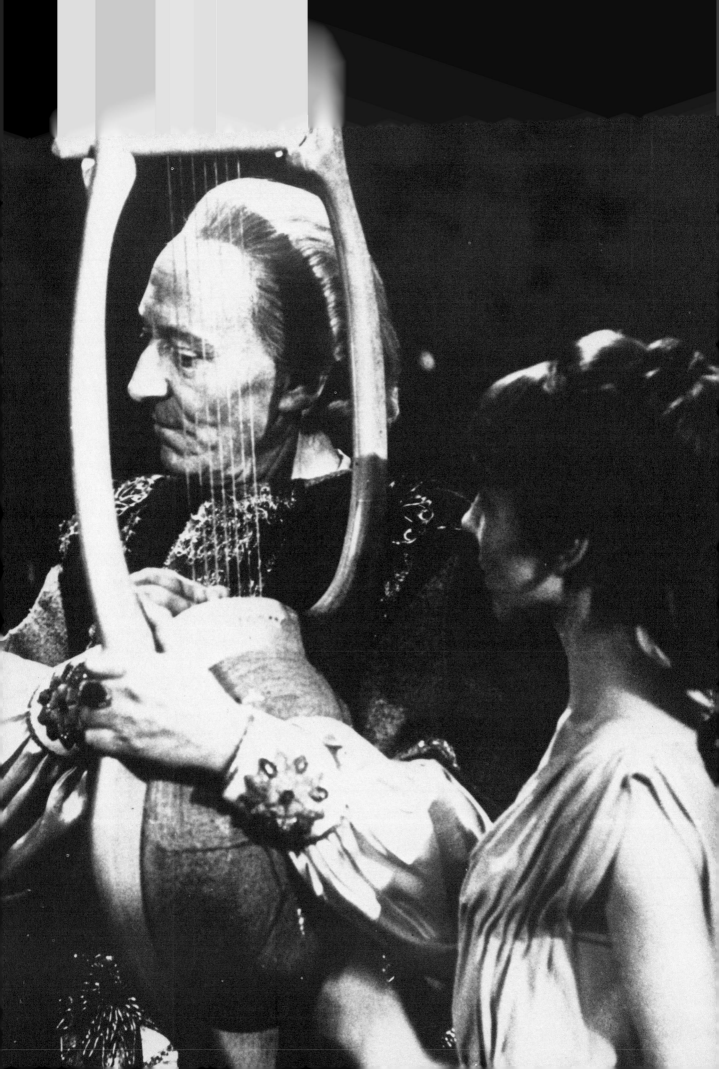

# THE ROMANS

The Cusick Stories
Serial 'M'

**Synopsis:** Just for a change the Doctor and his party have been able to relax and unwind awhile after so many strenuous adventures. The TARDIS has brought the time-travellers back to Roman times – to 64 AD to be exact – and they have been holidaying in a deserted villa near a small town.

But after several weeks of the idle life the Doctor is getting the 'exploration urge' again. Vicki too is anxious to see something of other worlds, times and places, and she persuades the Doctor to take her with him to Imperial Rome. Ian and Barbara, tired of hectic journeying, decide to remain at the villa.

No sooner have the Doctor and Vicki gone than the erstwhile school teachers are captured by slave traders who intend selling them at the slave markets in Rome. En route, the slavers make an early sale when Ian and two other prisoners are bought by the master of a galley ship.

At the slave auction there are many would-be buyers for Barbara, but she is eventually bought by the enigmatic Tavius, the keeper of the household at Nero's court.

151

"TURTLE SHELL LYRE" — MAKE 2/OFF :—
1/OFF FOR V·T·R· — 1/OFF FOR REHEARSALS —
— DRAWN HALF ACTUAL SIZE —

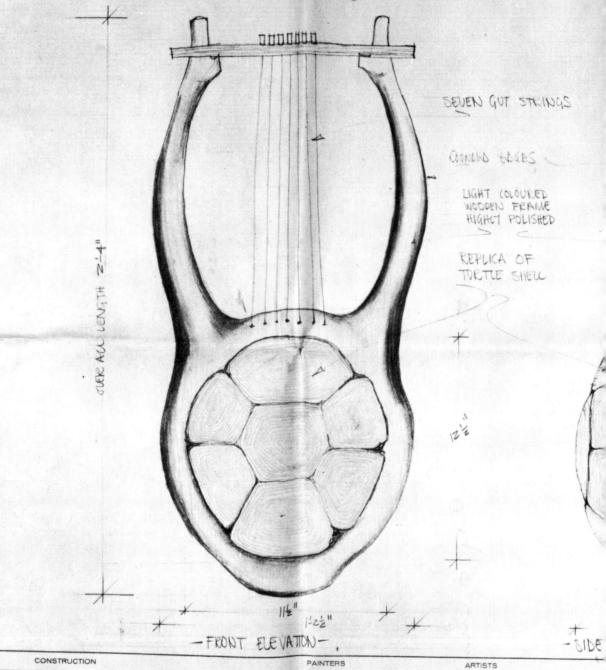

SEVEN GUT STRINGS

ROUNDED EDGES

LIGHT COLOURED
WOODEN FRAME
HIGHLY POLISHED

REPLICA OF
TURTLE SHELL

OVER ALL LENGTH 2'-4"

12½"

1½"
1'-2½"

— FRONT ELEVATION —

— SIDE

| CONSTRUCTION | PAINTERS | ARTISTS |
|---|---|---|

SPECIAL EFFECTS DRAWING — OUTSIDE CONTRACTOR —
SHAWCRAFT MODELS (UXBRIDGE) LIMITED —
DETAILS AS ABOVE AND AS DISCUSSED WITH DESIGNER —

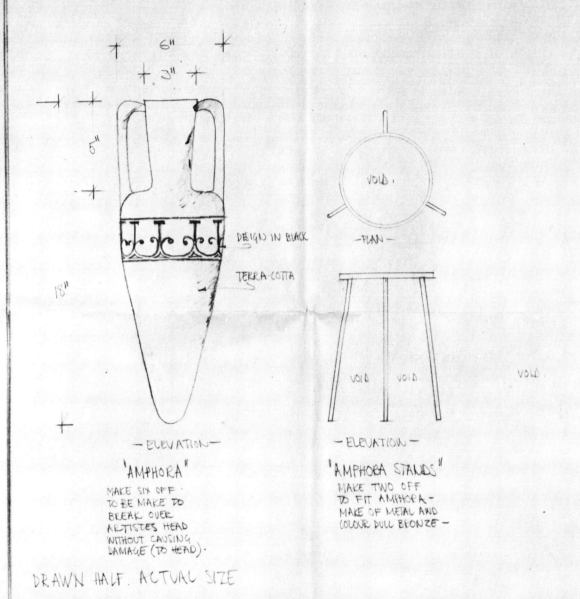

6"
3"
6"
18"

DESIGN IN BLACK

TERRA-COTTA

VOID.

— PLAN —

VOID    VOID.    VOID.

— ELEVATION —

— ELEVATION —

"AMPHORA"

MAKE SIX OFF
TO BE MAKE TO
BREAK OVER
ARTISTES HEAD
WITHOUT CAUSING
DAMAGE (TO HEAD).

"AMPHORA STANDS"

MAKE TWO OFF
TO FIT AMPHORA —
MAKE OF METAL AND
COLOUR DULL BRONZE —

DRAWN HALF. ACTUAL SIZE

STOCK

...OR SERIES ✳

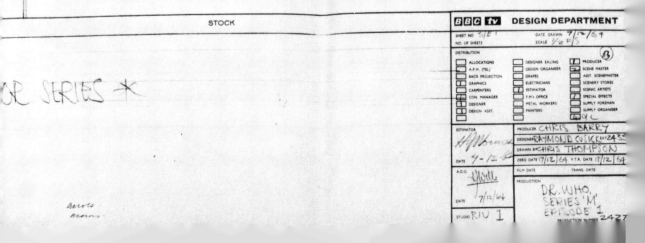

**BBC tv  DESIGN DEPARTMENT**

| | |
|---|---|
| SHEET NO. S/E 1 | DATE DRAWN 7/12/64 |
| NO. OF SHEETS | SCALE ½ F/S |

DISTRIBUTION

| | | |
|---|---|---|
| ALLOCATIONS | DESIGNER EALING | PRODUCER |
| A.P.H. (TEL) | DESIGN ORGANISER | SCENE MASTER |
| BACK PROJECTION | DRAPES | ASST. SCENEMASTER |
| GRAPHICS | ELECTRICIANS | SCENERY STORES |
| CARPENTERS | ESTIMATOR | SCENIC ARTISTS |
| CON. MANAGER | F.M's OFFICE | SPECIAL EFFECTS |
| DESIGNER | METAL WORKERS | SUPPLY FOREMAN |
| DESIGN ASST. | PAINTERS | SUPPLY ORGANISER |

| | |
|---|---|
| ESTIMATOR | PRODUCER CHRIS BARRY |
| | DESIGNER RAYMOND CUSICK EXT 2433 |
| | DRAWN BY CHRIS THOMPSON |
| DATE 7-12- | ZERO DATE 17/12/64  V.T.R. DATE 18/12/64 |
| A.D.O. | FILM DATE      TRANS. DATE |
| DATE 7/12/64 | PRODUCTION |
| STUDIO RIV 1 | DR. WHO. SERIES 'M' EPISODE 1 |
| | PRODUCTION NUMBER 2427 |

The Doctor and Vicki, meantime, have found out that all roads do indeed lead to Rome. Mistaken for the famous lyre player, Maximus Pettulian, the Doctor is invited to be a guest at Nero's court; an invitation he gleefully accepts until the daunting worry hits him that he might actually be expected to play (the Doctor cannot play a note).

A freak storm founders the slave galley manned by Ian, and he, along with a Greek named Delos, escape to the shore. They make their way to Rome where both are quickly recaptured and sent to the Gladiator School for training to meet the lions in the arena.

The Doctor, still mistaken for Pettulian, learns of a conspiracy against Nero in which the murdered lyre player was to play a major part. He decides, literally, to play for time and makes a debut at Nero's banquet that evening. Promising a passage of music so delicate that only those with keenly refined hearing will perceive it, the Doctor gives a recital – in total silence. With no-one wishing to appear insensitive or dull-witted the audience gives an enthusiastic response, thereby upsetting Nero.

Ian and Barbara meet – the latter having had a difficult time avoiding Nero's amorous advances – and with the help of Tavius (who is a Christian), they manage to escape from the city.

An accident involving the Doctor's glasses, the Emperor's plans for a new Rome, and the rays of the Sun, inspire Nero towards a drastic plan. If the Senate will not agree to his design for a new Rome, then he will burn down the present one and give them no choice. In the resulting Great Fire of Rome the Doctor and Vicki, like Ian and Barbara, slip away, each duo ignorant of the other's presence in the capital.

Ian and Barbara arrive back at the villa first, only to face the impossible task of trying to tell the Doctor and Vicki about their adventures while they are so full of their own. They agree to let their friends think they have just been 'lazing around'.

Ian and Delos (Peter Diamond) row for their lives as the galley runs into a storm.

**Background:** High farce came to *Doctor Who* with the writing of this story which author Dennis Spooner admits was heavily influenced by the then current fad for *Carry On . . .* films.

Spooner's idea came from an invitation by his actor-neighbour, Jim Dale, to visit the set of the latest *Carry On . . .* film at Pinewood – which just happened to be *Carry On Cleo*. Spotting an ideal target for a send-up, Dennis Spooner wrote his teleplay deliberately as a spoof of *Carry On Cleo* (which, in turn, was a spoof on *Quo Vadis*), even down to persuading Verity Lambert and Director Christopher Barry to hire some of the cast of the film, for example Gertan Klauber.

Ironically, the focal point of the story's humorous elements, comedian Derek Francis as Nero, was not Spooner's idea: Nero having died in his early thirties according to research. Francis was a close friend of Jacqueline Hill's husband, Producer/Director Alvin Rakoff, and had asked to be kept in mind for a part almost from *Doctor Who*'s beginning. With an eye to attracting 'bigger name' stars onto the show, Verity Lambert saw an opening for Francis as Nero and asked Spooner to write his personality into the scripts.

The storyline called for some expensive-sounding sequences, not the least being the burning of Rome, a galley ship foundering, and establishing shots of the Imperial capital. The latter two scenes were accomplished by negotiating rights, with Pinewood Studios, to use small segments from existing feature film footage.

For the burning of Rome shots, Ray Cusick, working on his

only historical *Doctor Who*, was lucky enough to pick up, quite by chance, an ex-exhibition architect's model of a colonnaded city which was then cremated on cue, with added flame effects overlaid on top of the recording to make the conflagration look even more spectacular.

Graduating from farce to slapstick, Stunt Arranger Peter Diamond (who also played Delos) devised and choreographed an extraordinarily energetic fight scene between William Hartnell and Barry Jackson (as the mute assassin Ascaris). Done in the best tradition of 'silent movies' it was a props fight featuring vases of water, curtain drapes and balsa wood chairs, ending with Ascaris voluntarily diving through the window to escape his tormentor.

Almost a case of history repeating itself, Episode Three ('Conspiracy') went out on air later than scheduled due to the death of a world-renowned statesman – in this case thanks to the lengthy coverage given to the funeral of Sir Winston Churchill on 30 January 1965.

This story is also notable for Mervyn Pinfield's last credit as Associate Producer for the series. His final contribution to *Doctor Who* was as Director on the four-part 'The Space Museum' story some months later.

156

The storm hits the galley which begins to founder.

OPPOSITE:
A centurion orders Ascaris to kill the Doctor . . .
. . . but the Doctor proves not that easy to kill . . .
. . . leaving Vicki to administer the crowning glory.

## Production Credits

Serial 'M'
Four Episodes
Black and White

| | |
|---|---|
| 'The Slave Traders' | 16 January 1965 |
| 'All Roads Lead to Rome' | 23 January 1965 |
| 'Conspiracy' | 30 January 1965 |
| 'Inferno' | 6 February 1965 |

### Cast

| | |
|---|---|
| Doctor Who | William Hartnell |
| Ian Chesterton | William Russell |
| Barbara Wright | Jacqueline Hill |
| Vicki | Maureen O'Brien |
| | |
| Sevcheria | Derek Sydney |
| Didius | Nicholas Evans |
| Centurion | Dennis Edwards |
| Stallholder | Margot Thomas |
| Slave Buyer | Edward Kelsey |
| Maximus Pettulian | Bart Allison |
| Ascaris | Barry Jackson |
| Delos | Peter Diamond |
| Tavius | Michael Peake |
| Woman Slave | Dorothy-Rose Gribble |
| Galley Master | Gertan Klauber |
| First Man in Market | Ernest Jennings |
| Second Man in Market | John Caesar |
| Court Messenger | Tony Lamden |
| Nero | Derek Francis |
| Tigilinus | Brian Proudfoot |
| Poppaea | Kay Patrick |
| Locusta | Ann Tirard |

### Crew

| | |
|---|---|
| Fight Arranger | Peter Diamond |
| Production Assistant | David Maloney |
| Assistant Floor Manager | Valerie Wilking |
| Lighting | Howard King |
| Sound | Richard Chubb |
| Costume Supervisor | Daphne Dare |
| Make-up Supervisor | Sonia Markham |
| Incidental Music | Raymond Jones |
| Story Editor | Dennis Spooner |
| Designer | Raymond P. Cusick |
| Associate Producer | Mervyn Pinfield |
| Producer | Verity Lambert |
| Director | Christopher Barry |

158

# THE CHASE

The Cusick Stories
Serial 'R'

**Synopsis:** Managing to repair the Time-Space Visualiser he acquired from the Space Museum, the Doctor affords his companions the unique opportunity of viewing history as it happened. For Ian he tunes in on Abraham Lincoln delivering the Gettysburg Address; Barbara chooses the court of Elizabeth I, watching Shakespeare and Bacon vying for posterity; and Vicki selects a 1965 performance by the Beatles, professing an interest in classical music.

The TARDIS materialises on a desert-covered, barren planet, with two fiercely burning suns. Ian and Vicki decide to explore as far as the next hill, leaving Barbara and the Doctor behind to sunbathe. As they bask under the twin suns they hear noises coming from the Visualiser. They are about to turn it off when a horrifying image swims into focus: an execution squad of Daleks is about to leave Skaro in a time-machine. Their mission is to pursue the TARDIS through time and space and to exterminate its crew for daring to interfere in Dalek plans.

Not knowing the vintage of this picture, the Doctor and Barbara

OVERLEAF:
A ground shot of the Mechonoids' magnificent city, towering on stilts above the jungle.

A Dalek emerges from its
time-machine into a 'haunted
house'.

set off in search of Ian and Vicki. But the Daleks are already here
and have commanded the planet's inhabitants – the Aridians – to
capture the travellers or be exterminated themselves. The
Aridians, locked in their own war for survival against savage Mire
Beasts, are in no position to oppose the Daleks and for a time the
TARDIS crew are their prisoners.

The time-travellers manage to escape from the Aridians and take
off in the TARDIS, but the Dalek time-ship is in hot pursuit.
Desperately, the Doctor tries a series of random landings in the
hope of eluding their pursuers. First they try the very top of the
Empire State Building, then the deck of an eighteenth-century
clipper – all to no avail. The Daleks are right behind them,
attacking any that stand in their way, including the crew of the
clipper, who hastily abandon ship. Only after both time-ships have
departed is the name *Mary Celeste* revealed.

A deserted Disneyland-style House of Horrors, populated by
ghosts, vampires and Frankenstein's monster, proves equally
useless in delaying or confusing the Daleks, and so reluctantly the
Doctor decides they must stand and fight.

On the planet Mechanus the time-travellers discover a
magnificent city on stilts populated by robots called Mechonoids,
who hold prisoner a man from Earth named Steven Taylor. There
is little time for introductions, however, as the Daleks attack the
city, determined to find the Doctor's group. Programmed to react
in kind, the Mechonoids turn on the Daleks, matching their ray
guns with supercharged flame throwers.

162

As Daleks and Mechonoids fight a mutual battle of annihilation, the humans escape down a rope to the jungle below, apparently losing Steven Taylor in the hasty retreat. Returning to the TARDIS they find the empty Dalek time-machine. Ian and Barbara use it to return to the 1960s at last, leaving Vicki and the Doctor to depart in the TARDIS.

**Background:** To prevent a rerun of problems encountered on 'The Keys of Marinus', two Designers were allocated to this serial to even out its massive effects and sets workload. Broadly speaking, John Wood handled the episodes on Aridius, the Empire State Building and the *Mary Celeste*, while Raymond Cusick oversaw the Haunted House and Mechanus episodes.

Cusick also devised the Dalek time-machine, an intricate contraption of revolving door panels designed to lose any impression of a visible interior. Like a magician's cabinet (on which it was based), any Dalek going through its portal would cause a series of panels to flip round, thereby giving the impression it had vanished without it being obvious how it had vanished.

The Dalek shape underwent some changes too. Not having worked on a Dalek story since the first one, Cusick was concerned that the creatures were apparently mobile outside their metal cities without any explanation as to how they were picking up power. He thus arranged to have each Dalek fitted with a waistband of vertical metal slats to suggest some form of solar ray receiving system.

But by far his main task on this story was the designing of the Mechonoids, or Mechons as the first scripts called them. Inspiration for their shape came from some of Buckminster Fuller's geodesic shapes and principles, coupled with some of the aviation structures devised by Barnes Wallis. *Shawcraft Models* were contracted to build the three robots the budget would allow, plus the model of their city on stilts. Ray Angel and Brian Hodgson were entrusted to come up with a suitably electronic-sounding voice.

Each Mechonoid was moulded in fibre-glass on a circular base and, like the Dalek, fitted with castors enabling it to roll along the floor. The operator inside was required to raise up, manually, the speech box lid mechanism and to actuate the three flashing lights whenever the robot spoke. He also had to work the two arm levers and extend the gun barrel on cue.

Unlike the Daleks, whose ray gun effects were supplied electronically, the Mechonoids actually had working flame throwers – hence why the battle scene in Episode Six had to be shot on film in the controlled environment of Ealing studios.

OVERLEAF:
The blueprints for the Mechonoids.

Seen as potential rivals to his Dalek creations, Terry Nation's Mechonoids proved too cumbersome to move easily around the studios.

The Mechonoids were intended to be the next 'big thing' from *Doctor Who* after the Daleks. A lot of promotion and merchandising was built up around them and, indeed, audience research showed they were very popular with children. The only people they were not popular with were studio production crews. The machines were just too big. In the confines of the small studios *Doctor Who* used for recording, they proved cumbersome

163

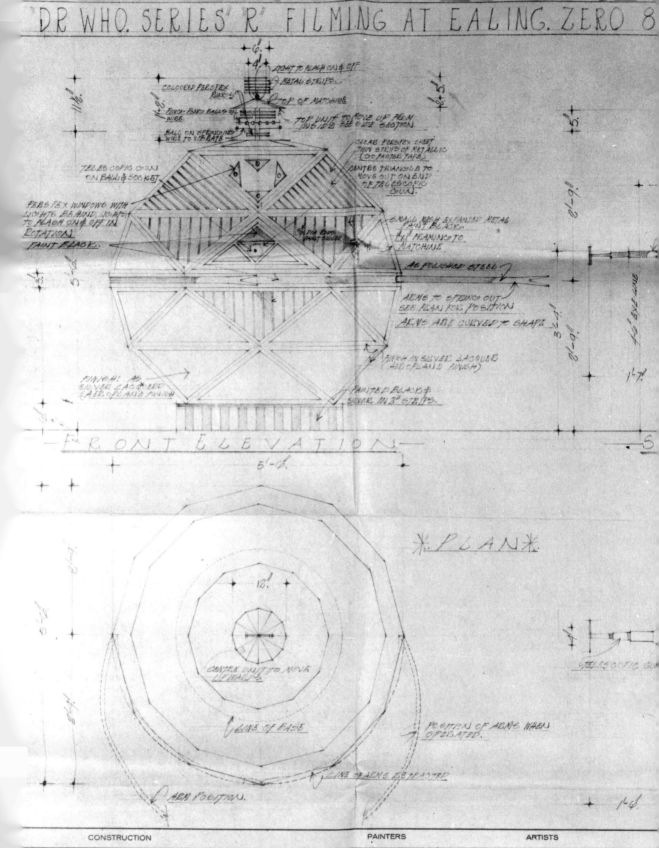

LIGHT TO FLASH ON & OFF

METAL STRIPS.

COLOURED PERSPEX DISC 5"

TOP OF MACHINE.

PING-PONG BALLS ON WIRE.

TOP UNIT TO MOVE UP FROM INSIDE BELOW SECTION.

BALL ON SPRINGING WIRE TO VIBRATE.

CLEAR PERSPEX SHEET THIN STRIPS OF METALLIC (00 PASTER TAPE.)

TELESCOPIC GUN ON BALL & SOCKET

CENTRE TRIANGLE TO MOVE OUT ON END OF TELESCOPIC GUN.

PERSPEX WINDOWS WITH LIGHTS BEHIND. LIGHTS TO FLASH ON & OFF IN ROTATION. PAINT BLACK.

SMALL MESH EXPANDED METAL PAINT BLACK.

½" FRAMING TO MACHINE.

AS POLISHED STEEL.

ARMS TO SWING OUT SEE PLAN FOR POSITION

ARMS ARE CURVED TO SHAPE

FINISH IN SILVER LACQUER (AEROPLANE FINISH)

FINISH: AS SILVER LACQUER (AEROPLANE FINISH)

PAINTED BLACK & SILVER IN 3" STRIPS.

## FRONT ELEVATION

5'-6.

## *PLAN*

18"

CENTRE UNIT TO MOVE UP & BACK

LINE OF BASE

POSITION OF ARMS WHEN OPERATED.

LINE OF ARMS RETRACTED

ARM POSITION.

TELESCOPIC GUN

| CONSTRUCTION | | PAINTERS | ARTISTS |
| --- | --- | --- | --- |

PLEASE NOTE: MAKE 3/MACHINES AS ABOVE FULLY PRAC.// TO BE ADAPTED (FOR FILMING.) FOR DISTRUCTION (WITH 4/REPEATS.

SPECIAL EFFECTS DRG, SHAWCRAFT (MODELS) LTD.,

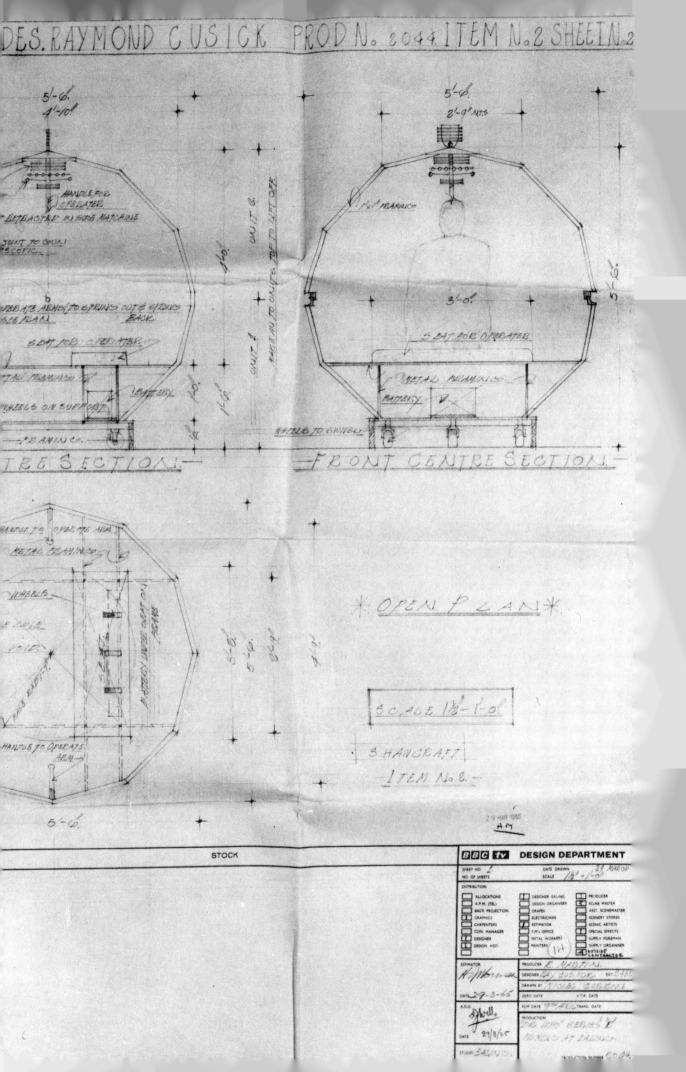

and unwieldy. As Script-Editor Dennis Spooner recalls, 'No-one could have stood the problems if they had caught on. They were just physically impossible to move in and out of the studios. Terry [Nation] was very unhappy about it.'

The Mechonoids appeared only in the last episode of 'The Chase' before they disappeared, never to be seen on Television again.

## Production Credits

Serial 'R'
Six Episodes
Black and White

| | |
|---|---|
| 'The Executioners' | 22 May 1965 |
| 'The Death of Time' | 29 May 1965 |
| 'Flight Through Eternity' | 5 June 1965 |
| 'Journey into Terror' | 12 June 1965 |
| 'The Death of Doctor | 19 June 1965 |
| Who' | 26 June 1965 |
| 'The Planet of Decision' | |

**Cast**

| | |
|---|---|
| Doctor Who | William Hartnell |
| Ian Chesterton | William Russell |
| Barbara Wright | Jacqueline Hill |
| Vicki | Maureen O'Brien |
| | |
| Abraham Lincoln | Robert Marsden |
| Francis Bacon | Roger Hammond |
| Queen Elizabeth I | Vivienne Bennett |
| William Shakespeare | Hugh Walters |
| Television Announcer | Richard Coe |
| Dalek Voices | Peter Hawkins, David Graham |
| Daleks | Robert Jewell, Kevin Manser, Gerald Taylor, John Scott-Martin |
| | |
| Ian Chesterton's Double | David Newman |
| Vicki's Double | Barbara Joss |
| Mire Beast | Jack Pitt |
| Malsan | Ian Thompson |
| Rynian | Hywel Bennett |
| Prondyn | Al Raymond |
| Walk-on Aridian | Brian Proudfoot |
| Guide | Arne Gordon |
| Morton Dill | Peter Purves |
| Albert C Richardson | Dennis Chinnery |
| Capt. Benjamin Briggs | David Blake Kelly |
| Bosun | Patrick Carter |
| Willoughby | Douglas Ditta |
| Cabin Steward | Jack Pitt |

| | |
|---|---|
| Walk-ons | Barbara Bruce, Kathleen Heath, Monique Lewis, Sean Ryan, Sally Sutherland, Jim Tyson, Bill Richards, Terry Leigh, David Pelton, Marc Lawrence |
| Stunt-men | Fred Haggerty, Gerry Wain, David Connon, Marilyn Gothard |
| Frankenstein | John Maxim |
| Count Dracula | Malcolm Rogers |
| Grey Lady | Roslyn De Winter |
| Robot Doctor Who | Edmund Warwick |
| Fungoids | John Scott Martin, Jack Pitt, Ken Tyllson |
| Mechonoid voice | David Graham |
| Mechonoids | John Scott Martin, Jack Pitt, Ken Tyllson |
| Steven Taylor | Peter Purves |
| Bus Conductor | Derek Ware |

**Crew**

| | |
|---|---|
| Fight Arranger | Peter Diamond |
| Production Assistants | Alan Miller, Colin Leslie |
| Assistant Floor Manager | Ian Strachan |
| Film Cameraman | Charles Parnall |
| Film Editor | Norman Matthews |
| Lighting | Howard King |
| Sound | Ray Angel |
| Costume Supervisor | Daphne Dare |
| Make-up Supervisor | Sonia Markham |
| Music | Dudley Simpson |
| Story Editor | Dennis Spooner |
| Designers | Raymond P. Cusick, John Wood |
| Producer | Verity Lambert |
| Director | Richard Martin |

# THE TIME MEDDLER

THE CLOCK on the gallery wall is edging past 8.25 pm. All around there is a buzz of nervous tension as everyone present prepares for the next one and a quarter hour's worth of pure adrenalin flow.

This is the story that has to be right. This is the story that caused all the fuss. This is the story that so nearly came to be cancelled. This is the story saved only by the unreadiness of the 'Journey to Cathay' serial scheduled to follow it. At last, after much debate, go-ahead has been finally, if somewhat reluctantly, given. Nevertheless, uppermost in the minds of Verity Lambert and David Whitaker, as they read through their copies of the camera script, must be thoughts of how heads could roll if this story ultimately fails to make the grade.

Down on the studio floor the mood can be likened to the kind of calm that precedes a storm. Where earlier in the day had prevailed an exercise in organised pandemonium – the sawing of wood for an extra set buttress, the clanking of lights being swung into position, and everywhere the ringing cacophony of cross conversation – now there is almost a deafening silence, broken only by the odd

Director Christopher Barry, as he appeared in his cameo shot in the 1976 story 'The Brain of Morbius', which starred Tom Baker as the Doctor.

apologetic cough as the minutes tick towards 8.30.

The cast, all in full costume, are standing near their initial cue points, eyes riveted on one man, the sweep of whose arm will tell them to start acting out the next episode of *Doctor Who*.

Many eyes are on this man, Production Assistant Norman Stewart (himself destined one day to direct *Doctor Who*). Seemingly standing rigid like a statue, his eyes are fixed on page one of the script while peripheral vision is trying to take in every detail of events going on around him in the studio. Uppermost in the priorities of his concentration are the voices coming through the headset he is wearing. For the next seventy-five minutes he will be the most important man on the floor – maintaining discipline and relaying all the instructions given him by the team assembled up in the gallery.

All four cameras scheduled for use in this episode are positioned on their 'A' positions, three of them aimed at the set on which the first scene will be acted out. The remaining one, set to one side, is trained on a large, easel-mounted blackboard on which the words, *DOCTOR WHO. SERIAL B. THE DEAD PLANET* have been chalked next to a clock-face. Not a conventional time-piece, this clock has a second hand only, recording each segment of a minute with solid, definite clicks.

One minute to go and the Director wishes everyone down on the floor good luck, and in time-honoured tradition Verity Lambert leans forward and wishes the Director good luck. For the next hour or more his will be the voice in command of *Doctor Who*, the one charged with the responsibility of turning words on a printed script into cans of videotape to be seen, weeks later, by the audience at home.

Seated next to the Director is the Production Secretary. As the minutes edge towards 8.30 she receives signals from all the technical stations. Lighting Control reports readiness, so too does Sound and Vision. Down in VT Control the machines bearing the master reels of 2″ videotape have been synchronously linked to the studio's cameras and stand all ready to run, this news too being passed up to the gallery of Studio D, Lime Grove.

For the man in the 'hot seat', Christopher Barry, this seven part serial will prove an important stepping stone in his chosen career as a Director, a career which began some sixteen years earlier on his leaving the armed forces.

In the Forties Britain still boasted a thriving film industry. Attracted by this, Barry applied to enter the film industry as an Assistant Director, only to be told this was impossible due to the closed shop enforced by the cinema union, ACCT. Looking around then for a non-union post he succeeded in getting an appointment to the Script Department at Ealing Studios, a complex famous the world over for its comedies. Once in, Barry was able to amass experience in film-making to a point where he could apply, with confidence of success, for the much-needed union ticket. That acquired, he gained rapid promotion to Second Assistant Director, and then to First Assistant Director.

Barry remembers his time at Ealing as a period of intense

170

learning: 'It was very much a team effort there, with an awful lot of give and take. At *The Red Lion* across the road criticism and encouragement of one's colleagues, by one's colleagues, was the norm, which I think was a wholly creative process, and which is, sadly, somewhat lacking at the BBC.

'Very often, at Ealing, the Director himself would think up ideas for films and would probably have a lot to do with the genesis of the scripts as well.'

By the early Fifties, however, it was apparent the movie industry in Britain was beginning to run out of steam, losing ground to a younger, more immediate industry with which it just could not compete – Television. Throughout 1954 and 1955 the setting up of ITV led to a great exodus of talent from the BBC, attracted, no doubt, by the higher rates of pay advertised by the commercial stations. The result was a big recruitment drive mounted by the Corporation across a wide parallel of jobs to fill the vacuums. Spotting the light of prospect, Christopher Barry applied to join the BBC, and came in as a Production Assistant in 1955. Straight away though, despite the technical wizardry of the medium, he found it had its limitations.

'At that time, and to a large extent even now, Television was very much based in Theatre. There was a lot of use of film, but with the exception of people like Alan Bromly, who had worked in movies, few knew how to make best use of it. Coming in from a film background myself, and being film-minded, I found I was soon in demand to help out with film sequences – ultimately being asked to direct these sequences for Directors who didn't have much experience with the medium.'

As the 1950s became the 1960s, the big limitation of television programme making, which so restricted Directors versed in the film world, came to be the technique of Continuous Recording, whereby productions were done, as far as possible, like theatrical plays; beginning at Act One, Scene One, and running sequentially through to the end. Part of this was a hang over from the days of live Television, but even as the Fifties turned into the Sixties, and prerecording came into the limelight, the cost and cumbersome nature of videotape ruled out all but the most rudimentary of editing.

'The stopping and cutting of tape was always said to be very expensive, not only in the cost of the tape but also in the man hours needed to do it. You certainly wasted studio time and resources, so one was actively discouraged. In fact at various times there would be BBC rulings issued down concerning the number of breaks you could have in a recording, so you had to choose your breaks with great discretion to make best use of them.

'This obviously led, in some ways, to a cramping of style. To move a character from set A to set B you needed to write in a short bridging scene, the effect of which was to stretch out the script with padding, which was not always the best thing for the story. Correspondingly with over-runs, because editing was frowned upon, if you had things you wanted to cut out you couldn't do it so easily. For instance you couldn't, like nowadays, tighten up a slack scene where people weren't picking up their cues so quickly by cutting out a few pauses here and there.

'It's easy to edit now electronically, but in those days, where editing was done by looking down a microscope for a metal ink pulse, cutting the tape physically with a guillotine and then joining edges together with sticky tape, it took a very long time and could be very wasteful.'

'Dries' and 'line fluffs' were also actively discouraged for similar reasons. During the days of live Television AFMs were equipped with a 'cut key' – a hard-wired push-button which, when pressed, cut off all sound from the studio microphones so that the viewers at home could not hear the prompt line being called out by the AFM. Even after the adoption of prerecording, 'cut keys' were still used, the artist being encouraged to carry on acting in character until the prompt was given, thereby reducing editing time. 'Cut keys' were modified during the late Fifties to substitute studio atmospherics instead of dead silence, on the assumption that studio background 'mush' sounded more natural than absolute muting.

All these problems, and a good deal more, were faced by those drama Directors whose programmes were scheduled for production using Lime Grove's facilities. Studio D especially, Christopher Barry remembers as being, 'very much smaller than most studios at Television Centre, certainly very much lower in height, which meant the lamps were down lower as well, and therefore hotter for the actors and crew. It was very, very cramped which meant you had sets one on top of another. You tended not to have room to use cameras on cranes, so you had to rely on pedestals just to get them in there. And Lime Grove had big, heavy, lumbering cameras with turrets on the front, so you had to check positioning very carefully.

'It meant a lot of work for the Director preparing his camera script because he had to know exactly where to put his cameras to get the shots he wanted. We used to work with protractors on paper, measuring out the four angles viewable through each of the turret lenses. So when you got to see the Designer's scale model of the studio sets you knew that if you wanted to put an actor in one spot, in mid-shot, camera one would have to be precisely in such-and-such position with one lens, camera two would have to be precisely in another position with another lens, and so on. There was no hit and miss about it as can happen today where you can put a camera virtually anywhere and zoom into the position for any shot you want. Everything had to be worked out with great precision. Indeed I think it is true to say the technical know-how required then was far greater than it is now.

'To give an illustration, I can remember working with one very eminent Director, Julian Aymes, as his Production Assistant. He was so precise with his camera positions at outside rehearsal that, literally, before I left the church hall, or whatever we were using, to come into the studio I would measure off, with string and a compass, co-ordinates from the front edge of the marked-out set to each of his floor indicated camera positions. I could then plot that

ABOVE:
Film cameraman Peter Hamilton and Christopher Barry (in hat) shooting location material for 'The Savages'.

BELOW:
Christopher Barry, Peter Purves as the Doctor's companion, Steven, and Chal (Ewen Solon) relax between takes on 'The Savages'.

172

precise position again when I got into the studio as the spot for a camera and, by Jove, he was always right.

'With Lime Grove then, if you were planning a long shot from any particular place you had to be sure the camera could physically get to that exact spot to take it.

'Another factor you had to reckon with was the time needed to change a lens on the camera turret. If you wanted to cut from a wide shot to a close-up, you had to cut away to another camera long enough for the lens to be swung round into position and refocussed. Quite often, if you weren't careful, you'd cut back and the lens would still be swinging and focusing up.'

The assigning of Christopher Barry to direct the first Dalek serial stemmed from a direct invitation by Verity Lambert to do so. Such was the set up of the Drama Department in the Sixties that a staff Production Assistant could find himself being allowed a turn in the Director's chair for one show, giving directions to a fellow PA colleague, and then, a few months' later be taking directions from perhaps that same PA, whose turn it had now become to be elevated to the directing heights. Between 1955 and 1964 Barry's job title remained that of a Production Assistant even though, throughout most of the early Sixties, he was spending more and more time in the Director's seat, only narrowly missing, through his own admitted naivety, the golden opportunity of directing Donald Wilson's great opus, *The Forsyte Saga*.

With his film background, Verity Lambert saw in Barry a good technical brain, ingenious enough to overcome *Doctor Who*'s limited budget through inventiveness and by optimum use of what special effects were available at the time.

Continuous recording drastically limited a lot of standard studio effects taken for granted years later. To dematerialise the TARDIS from Paleolithic Earth, for example, Waris Hussein had resorted to using a process involving a 'caption slide mix'.

Using this technique required one camera pointed at the live set, another pointed at an easel bearing a large, mounted photograph – a caption slide. For the dematerialisation shot the caption slide needed to be of the deserted landscape, ie: with the TARDIS gone. The live set would feature the TARDIS, so by careful aligning of two camera positions and angles the two pictures on the output monitor could be made exactly the same, with only the TARDIS prop showing which one was which. Therefore, at recording time, all that was needed to dematerialise the ship was a simple mix from the camera pointing at the live set to the camera aimed at the caption slide.

Richard Martin, for the ending of the Dalek show, adopted a different technique. With an eye on the number of recording breaks he could schedule, he elected to use one to do a 'locked-off roll-back and mix'. Using this method one camera alone was needed to shoot the TARDIS on the live set, firstly locking all its settings as the time-travellers go inside and then fading out its picture from the output monitor. After that came the break, during which time the TARDIS prop would be moved ('struck' in studio terminology), and the videotape of the previous shot rewound. On recommencing shooting the same locked-off camera would hold its picture of the empty set, that shot then being mixed with the replay, producing a finished recording of the ship apparently fading away while the background remains stable.

The other major electronic effect employed in *Doctor Who* during its early life was Inlay, a fairly rudimentary form of matting which allowed the picture from one camera to be placed – inlaid – into the picture from another.

The opening episode of 'The Daleks', 'The Dead Planet' premiers the use of Inlay in *Doctor Who* for one of the most historic shots in the programme's history – the awesome moment when the Doctor, Ian, Barbara and Susan first look down at the glittering towers of the Dalek city, gleaming, some miles distant, in the rays of the setting sun.

Constructed by *Shawcraft Models* to Ray Cusick's exact specifications, the Dalek city was a fairly sizeable, tabletop model some twenty-five foot square. As it would not fit into the studio, and also to soften the image, and hence give it a greater depth of field, Ray Cusick and Christopher Barry agreed to have all the shots of the model done on film, realising that video would show definition too harshly, making the model look too much like a model.

To do the Inlay shot required mixing film footage of the city with live action of the Doctor's party. This, in turn, required a gallery-controlled Telecine Transfer.

Telecine Transfer is the recording of film onto tape, normally done in the Telecine Department, but also capable of being fed up to the gallery where a small desk-top electronic camera is set up to record the footage. To all intents and purposes this camera's output is treated the same as that from any of the cameras down on the studio floor, and can be manipulated accordingly.

Up in the 'Fish Tank' is an area set aside for the Inlay Operator, still many years away from his grander title of Electronic Effects Designer. His equipment is a flat, white topped desk with an electronic rostrum camera mounted above it. Inside the camera is a logic mechanism keyed to register the colours black and white. Where the camera sees white it sends to the output monitor the picture seen by Camera A, where it sees black it sends out Camera B's picture.

For the Dalek city distance shot, Camera A is the desk-top Telecine Transfer camera, which will run footage of the Dalek city model. Camera B is one of the floor cameras, shooting the Doctor and his companions against a cliff background.

With a pair of scissors the Inlay Operator cuts out a small piece of black card which he places on his white desktop. The black cut-out being shaped to suggest a cliff ledge.

Switched through to the output monitor, the resulting composite picture shows the Dalek city model as the main picture (Camera A's shot) with a small, bottom-right inset, replacing the black area, of the Doctor's group standing as though they were on a cliff ledge.

Another electronic effect, pioneered for this story, and

thereafter used in all subsequent Dalek serials, was the Dalek extermination effect – a very simple trick of opening a camera's aperture too wide, thereby admitting in too much light, swamping the camera's electronics and causing it to send back to the gallery a negative image.

Later on, in the episode 'The Ambush' both Inlay and the extermination effect were blended to show the devastating result of a Dalek blaster on full power. In this case a length of film footage showing a melting strip of metal was inlaid into the picture of a Dalek city corridor. Timed in with the picture dipping into negative the finished shot impressively demonstrated a wall apparently buckling and melting under Dalek firepower.

By such combinations of ingenuity, skill, adrenalin and resourcefulness the early *Doctor Who* serials were put into the can, needing a minimum of post-production work to get them ready for transmission. What is truly remarkable, though, was the speed at which the episodes were turned out. At 8.30 pm on most Fridays of the year recording began on a new episode. By 9.45 pm, 10.00 pm at the very latest, a full episode was in the can, complete with its opening and closing title graphics, all the incidental music, all optical and mechanical effect sequences, even the strange and wierd electronic voices of such monsters as the Daleks and the Mechonoids.

For Christopher Barry, involvement with the first Dalek story began some months earlier, on a day referred to as Director Joining Date. By then it was expected a set of scripts for that show would be available in rehearsal form for the Director to peruse, assess and add his contribution. In reality, full scripts are seldom ready in finished form by this date, especially on serials where the pressures on the Script Editor, who is handling a whole team of writers, are extreme.

With this story too came the added responsibility of co-directorship, Christopher Barry sharing his task with ex-Theatre Director Richard Martin who was scheduled to shoot three of the seven episodes.

Meetings then followed. Many of them, beginning principally with the Production Designer, Raymond Cusick, in whose hands rest the visual look of the story, from the smallest prop to the biggest backdrop, and especially of the design and handling of the Daleks themselves.

More discussions: with Costume and Make-Up supervisors on the outfitting of the actors, with lighting experts who must disguise the limited dimensions of Lime Grove, and particularly with Sound Engineers, in this case with Ray Angel who was asked to devise a special voice for the Dalek aliens.

Having the added bonus of a symbiosis with Richard Martin, but with the advantage of handling the first few episodes himself, Barry's memory is of an intensely creative period in the weeks before his first studio session on 'The Daleks'.

'With Richard, he learned from me, and I learned from him. Our ideas coalesced with those of Ray Cusick in the production of the Dalek itself once we'd all seen the scripts. The script gave one a hint of what they were all about, but after that it was a question of backwards and forwards passing of sketches, ideas on backs of envelopes, bits of paper until ultimately we came down to this pepper-pot shape which Ray then had to translate into something which could be manipulated and made to work – which he did brilliantly.

'Were they being designed afresh today I've no doubt they'd be done quite differently. Certainly the lack of skill we encountered synchronising the flashing light bulbs with the voice patterns was not terribly successful in that quite often they were way out of phase.

'We did manage to achieve Dalek eye contact with our actors by devising a kind of iris round for one of the cameras which gave you a point-of-view shot from the Dalek. In the very first episode I did, we fitted that onto a wobbling camera tracking in (today you'd call it a hand-held shot) and, together with a sucker cup sticking out into shot, it gave you an impression of the thing lumbering towards Barbara down a passage. I then subsequently asked for an iris to be put into the Dalek so that we could do a close up of the eye irising in and out to get the effect of its eye focussing on you.

'For the Dalek voice we arranged a special experimental session in one of the sound galleries so that Ray Angel could play back to us several test treatments he'd come up with to see what we thought. Eventually we all agreed we wanted this fierce bark that was both harsh and metallic, after which it was just a case of refining it down until we settled on the precise tone we ended up using.

'Fairly early on we decided we'd have separate people doing the Dalek voices because the actors hired to work them from the inside were being engaged more for their physical skills in manipulating Daleks than for their formal acting abilities, made redundant by the energies just to operate them.'

Having started the design ball rolling and given himself some idea of cast requirements, Barry moved on to his foremost task – that of constructing the camera script.

Receiving a script, which bears all the writer's material on the right hand side of the page, the Director's stage directions to his cameras and microphones go on the left hand side. In writing these notes a good many questions must be borne in mind all the time. What type of shot is he looking for? Where must a camera be to achieve this shot? What other cameras are needed for this scene? Can one, maybe two cameras, be moved to the next set for the following scene? Does the script allow a smooth transition from one scene to another without a recording break? Or, must some bridging material be built in to allow cameras or cast time to get to the next set? Is there enough time left in one scene to allow time to set up an Inlay shot using two cameras on the next scene? Is this speech long enough on one camera to allow another camera time to switch lenses for a medium shot? Does this sequence need to be done on film? Will the budget allow us to have that many Daleks in an episode? All in all, hundreds of questions of logistics and choreography, all needing to be answered before the one crucial studio recording session commences.

Rehearsal time for the cast would be limited, just a few days together in a church hall with sticky tape on the floor and a few odd props to suggest sets that will only be seen on the Friday.

Any film sequences need to be shot in advance, ready for Telecine Transfer on the date of recording. Similarly any prerecorded voices, sound effects and incidental music needed to be prepared and in the hands of the Grams Operator, in order of cueing, before zero hour on the big day.

Finally, all is prepared and as the second hand ticks over into 8.30 pm the command 'Run Tape' is given.

At this signal the master tape is run up to speed, an okay then being passed back to the Director by the Technical Manager. Telecine now gets the direction to run the first piece of 16mm film – the familiar opening graphics sequence together with the sound-on-film theme music. Mixing after 20 seconds the next sequence is also a piece of film on a second playback machine, recorded from Waris Hussein's last episode: a recapitulation of the previous episode's cliff-hanger as the TARDIS's radiation counter edges into the Danger Zone.

Now the action moves to the studio floor. Two cameras, switched to give an almost negative image that enhances the metallic quality of the foliage (and presaging the Dalek gunfire effect mentioned earlier), pan across the ashen forest in sweeping arcs, their pictures mixed together giving a greater impression of size to the dense, white foliage. Output from a third camera is faded in – the one shooting caption slides of 'The Dead Planet', and *Written by Terry Nation*. During this establishing sequence the Grams Operator's first duty is to fade up a track of Tristram Cary's incidental mood effects to go with the establishing shots.

Finally output is switched back to the second camera which is focussed on the forest clearing. At a cue from the Director the PA sweeps his hand down, indicating a 'Go' to the cast frozen like statues just outside the camera's field of vision.

As the Doctor, Susan, Ian and Barbara emerge and enter the clearing the other three cameras shift to their second shooting spots. The camera holding the action switches slowly to a normal, positive picture – more acceptable to viewers now that the impact has been made. The other cameras do likewise. Once all the correct lenses have been swung into place and focussing is complete, the initial dialogue between the time-travellers can be made more interesting by switching between close-ups, mid-shots, group shots, etc.

Stepping forward to the front of the jungle set, actor William Russell places himself so that the windflow from a small cooling fan falls on his face, ruffling his hair slightly as Ian Chesterton remarks on the slight breeze blowing over this exotic world. Up in the gallery a careful watch is being kept on sound levels to ensure the noise from the fan is drowned out by the radiophonic wind effect now carrying through the studio's talkback system and being picked up by the microphones.

As dialogue continues down on the floor the Inlay Operator

178

prepares for the first of his 'big moments'; the establishing shot of the city as seen by the time-travellers. During camera rehearsals earlier in the day he was able to cut out, align and stick down his black cardboard mask. With this in position he waits for the right moment to switch through the distance shot film of the city, coupled with the live action inlay of the characters.

A short bridging scene has been included between Susan and Barbara to allow a camera time to get onto its marks and change lenses for the Inlay shot. This gives the Inlay Operator a vital few moments to check the lining-up of his shot. Is the cut-out mask affixed correctly? Is the Telecine Transfer film of the city being run up on cue? Does the angle of the composite shot look right? A slip-up now and an extra, unscheduled recording break will be necessary.

Inevitably there must be one or two recording breaks. The scene where Susan runs into Ian, having been tapped on the shoulder by an unseen hand (in truth that of AFM Michael Ferguson, later, too, to become a *Doctor Who* Director), is followed directly by a sequence in the TARDIS with all four time-travellers. Recording needs to be paused here to allow William Russell and Carole Ann Ford time to join the others on the TARDIS set.

By contrast, however, no halting of equipment is needed between the night-time scene in the TARDIS, and the following 'next day' scene. A simple fade-to-black (a common technique used in the Sixties) gives the artists a few vital seconds to reposition themselves before the fade-up suggests action happening the following morning. An edit will cut this pause (called a 'run on') down to perhaps just a second on the finished version of the episode.

Scenes in the Dalek city sets are slightly trickier. The script identifies the city as a vast 'magical architecture'. Yet it too must fit into the confines of Studio D. To increase its apparent depth several backdrops have been added to the sets, including one to make the corridors seem much longer. Camera angling for these shots must be very precise to match the perspective view the scenic artist has painted on the backdrop.

Similarly, the Dalek city sets feature many 'working props' – remotely controlled camera eyes, power-operated metal doors, even a lift. The illusion of Television and some precise cueing by the PA must disguise the fact that all these props are being moved to order by stage hands hidden behind the sets.

Thankfully, everything goes smoothly. As the hour ticks towards 9.45 pm the final shot is recorded. One camera, taking the simile to a Dalek too closely, trundles towards Barbara, an iris cowl over its lens and a Dalek sucker cup waving in front of it. Backing against a wall she screams a scream that will soon have most of Britain in suspense, and the output cuts to a camera facing the roller caption machine on which the end credits are being displayed. The theme music is faded up by the Grams Operator, and then faded down again after the final credit has been captured on tape.

The next episode of *Doctor Who* is in the can.

# MISSION TO THE UNKNOWN

The Cusick Stories
Serial 'T/A'

**Synopsis:** In the jungles of the most hostile planet in the Galaxy, two men are desperately trying to repair a small rocket ship. They are Marc Cory and Captain Gordon Lowery. The latter is angry with Cory for chartering his rocket and ordering him to fly here without word of explanation. Now, after a perilous landing, there is considerable doubt if the craft will ever fly again.

This heated debate ends when the third member of the crew, pilot Jeff Garvey, emerges from the surrounding bushes, driven by an overwhelming desire to kill Lowery. Calmly Cory shoots him down. He shows the Captain where Garvey had been stung by a Varga thorn, a venomous biological creation found on only one planet in the skies . . . As the two men climb aboard the ship, Garvey's body begins to transform into a Varga – a half-animal, half-vegetable creature armed with poison thorns and covered with coarse, white hair.

Cory reveals his identity as a member of Space Security. The Daleks, he explains, have gained control of a vast area of the ninth galaxy, plus the constellation of Miros. These are millions of light

OVERLEAF:
Marc Cory's distress rocket, which he intended to launch into orbit to warn the solar system of the Daleks' threat.

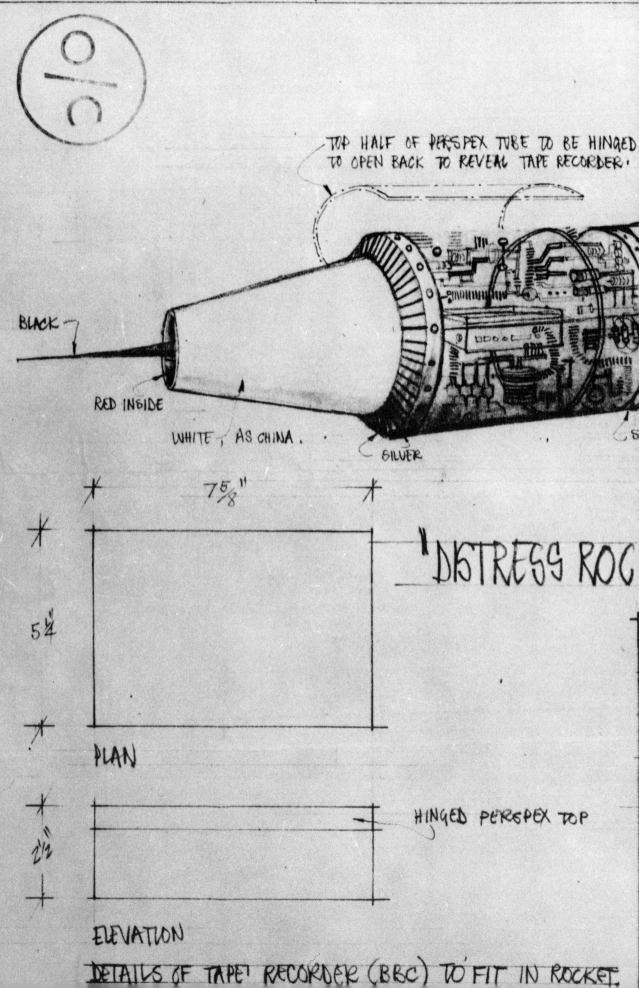

O/C

TOP HALF OF PERSPEX TUBE TO BE HINGED
TO OPEN BACK TO REVEAL TAPE RECORDER.

BLACK

RED INSIDE

WHITE , AS CHINA .

SILVER

S

7⅝"

" DISTRESS ROC

5¼"

PLAN

HINGED PERSPEX TOP

2½"

ELEVATION

DETAILS OF TAPE RECORDER (BBC) TO FIT IN ROCKET

# 15. DESIGNER RAY CUSICK · PROD Nº 2187

## ·SPECIAL EFFECTS DRAWING·

RED FINS WITH WHITE LETTERING

D.S.F.G.1

BLACK

FINISH AS CHROME

TAPE RECORDER
(BBC.)

12"

9"

4"

2"
1"

15"
PERSPEX
TUBE

1"

2'-0"

ELEVATION 1"-1'-0" SCALE

6" 3½"

KEEP FOR SERIES

AS ABOVE & AS DISCUSSED
E SPECIAL EFFECT
ACTOR:-
NCRAFT MODELS
RIDGE) LTD.

RECEIVED
16 JUL 1965
DESIGN
MANAGER

O/C

### BBC tv  DESIGN DEPARTMENT

| SHEET NO. S/E | DATE DRAWN 16 JULY |
| NO. OF SHEETS | SCALE 1"-1'-0" |

**DISTRIBUTION**

| | | |
|---|---|---|
| ☐ ALLOCATIONS | ☐ DESIGNER EALING | ☑ PRODUCER |
| ☐ A.P.M. (TEL) | ☐ DESIGN ORGANISER | ☑2 SCENE MASTER |
| ☐ BACK PROJECTION | ☐ DRAPES | ☐ ASST. SCENEMASTER |
| ☑ GRAPHICS | ☐ ELECTRICIANS | ☐ SCENERY STORES |
| ☐ CARPENTERS | ☑ ESTIMATOR | ☐ SCENIC ARTISTS |
| ☐ CON. MANAGER | ☐ F.M's OFFICE | ☑ SPECIAL EFFECTS |
| ☑ DESIGNER | ☐ METAL WORKERS | ☐ SUPPLY FOREMAN |
| ☑ DESIGN ASST. | ☐ PAINTERS  ⑫ | ☐ SUPPLY ORGANISER |
| ☐ | ☐ | ☑ O/C |

| ESTIMATOR | PRODUCER DEREK MARTINUS |
| | DESIGNER RAY CUSICK  EXT 2435 |
| | DRAWN BY CHRIS THOMPSON |
| DATE | ZERO DATE AUG 5   V.T.R. DATE AUG 6 |
| A.D.O. | FILM DATE   TRANS. DATE |
| | PRODUCTION |
| DATE 16/7/65 | DR WHO SERIES T/A EPISODE 1 OF 1 |
| STUDIO TC4 | PRODUCTION NUMBER 2187 |

years away from both the Solar System and here, yet a week before, a freighter captain saw a Dalek space ship very close to this world – Kembel.

Nursing a hunch that Kembel, avoided by all other space traffic, might be the Dalek's base, Cory chartered Lowery's vessel for this exploratory trip. Garvey's condition has confirmed his opinion. The Varga Plants, a wound from whose thorns replaces a man's thoughts with an overwhelming urge to kill and turns him into one of themselves, grow naturally only on the planet whose laboratories have developed them: Skaro, home of the Daleks.

At the nearby Dalek outpost preparations are being made to receive emissaries from seven planets, and orders are given by the Black Dalek to hunt down and exterminate the Earthmen known to have landed on Kembel.

The rocket cannot be repaired in time so Cory and Lowery, with message-sending equipment, make their escape through the jungle as the Daleks close in. Seeking a clearing, from which to launch a message into space, they watch as an enormous space ship from an outer galaxy passes overhead.

Cory discovers the enemy city, and learns that the Solar System is to be invaded and destroyed. Returning to the jungle he finds he has to kill Lowery who has been stung by a Varga. Quickly he records a message of warning, but before he can launch it the Daleks locate and kill him. The message rolls away on the ground.

In the conference hall the seven great powers from the outer galaxies pledge their allegiance to the Dalek cause, and agree to join in the greatest war force ever assembled. Their first target will be the Earth.

The Daleks' Master Plan has begun.

**Background:** 'Mission to the Unknown' stands unique in the annals of *Doctor Who*, being the only story, albeit a one-episode story, where the star of the show was not the actor playing the title role. For one week Edward de Souza was accorded top billing, playing Marc Cory very akin to Sean Connery's all-conquering interpretation of James Bond. Neither William Hartnell, Maureen O'Brien nor Peter Purves appeared in this episode for a complex set of reasons traceable right back to 'Planet of Giants'.

The second season of *Doctor Who* was originally scheduled to run forty-four weeks as a continuous serial, giving way thereafter to an eight week break before, presumably, a third season.

Already a decision had been made, sometime in 1964, to hive 'Planet of Giants' and 'The Dalek Invasion of Earth' off from the first season – in whose block they had been recorded – and to graft them as openers to the second season, thus giving the overworked Production Office a bit of a breather.

Then, fairly close to transmission, Verity Lambert decided to tighten the dramatic structure of 'Planet of Giants' by truncating it from four episodes to three. This correspondingly gave rise to a hole in the planned running length of the second season and was discussed at Department head level some months later. Sydney Newman duly filled the hole by granting *Doctor Who* an extra

episode to replace the one lost.

This, however, presented Verity Lambert with a problem. Although the viewers would still see the planned number of episodes, production-wise it meant re-engaging the regular cast for an extra week's recording: potentially expensive as contracts would need to be re-negotiated.

Her solution was the innovative idea of a one-episode teaser to presage the planned epic length 'The Daleks' Master Plan' serial. That way, the regular cast could keep their holiday time, and the season could end on an exciting 'To Be Continued . . .' note. But in the tradition of all best laid plans, subsequent events overturned this scheme.

Somewhat late in the day BBC Programme Planning decided it was unhappy with new seasons of *Doctor Who* opening around early November. Far better, they said, if it formed part of the Autumn Season package unveiled in September. Hence *Doctor Who*'s second series got shortened to thirty-nine weeks, ending with 'The Time Meddler' instead.

'Mission to the Unknown' also marked the departure of Verity Lambert as Producer of the series. She had spent two years solidly on the programme and felt now was a good time for a change. Sydney Newman agreed, already having a replacement project in mind for her. The project in question was *Adam Adamant Lives*, a less fantastic, if still fantasy-based, series about another time-traveller who comes out of suspended animation from 1902 into the 'Swinging London' world of 1965.

Lambert's successor on *Doctor Who* was former in-house Script Editor John Wiles, strongly recommended to Sydney Newman by Donald Wilson from their days together in the Script Department. Wiles, it was hoped, would restore the intended seriousness to *Doctor Who*, which he felt had been lost somewhat in the wake of the Daleks' success.

**Production Credits**

Serial 'T/A'
One Episode
Black and White

'Mission to the                 9 October 1965
Unknown'

**Cast**
Marc Cory                       Edward De Souza
Jeff Garvey                     Barry Jackson
Gordon Lowery                   Jeremy Young
Malpha                          Robert Cartland
Trantis                         Ronald Rich
Daleks                          Robert Jewell, Kevin Manser, John
                                Scott-Martin, Gerald Taylor
Dalek Voices                    David Graham, Peter Hawkins
Varga Plants                    Tony Starn, Roy Reeves, Leslie
                                Weeks
Planetarians                    Johnny Clayton, Pat Gorman, Sam
                                Mansary, Len Russell

**Crew**
Production Assistant            Angela Gordan
Assistant Floor Manager         Majorie Yorke
Costume Supervisor              Daphne Dare
Make-up Supervisor              Sonia Markham
Story Editor                    Donald Tosh
Designers                       Richard Hunt
                                Raymond P. Cusick
Producer                        Verity Lambert
Director                        Derek Martinus

# THE DALEKS' MASTER PLAN

The Cusick Stories
Serial 'V'

**Synopsis:** The year is 4000 AD, and the Solar System is at peace under its guardian Mavic Chen. But on the planet Kembel, Space Security agent Bret Vyon has unearthed evidence that the Daleks plan to attack Earth and acquire the Solar System as the first move in their overall ambition to rule the entire Universe.

The Doctor, the injured Steven, and the handmaiden Katarina from Troy, land on Kembel. While the Doctor goes to find help for Steven, Bret attempts to hijack the TARDIS, but is thwarted. Explaining the situation, Bret enlists the Doctor's help and, together with Katarina and a recovering Steven, they manage to steal the core of the most evil machine ever devised, the Time Destructor. The Daleks have surrounded the TARDIS, so the time-travellers are forced to make their escape in the space yacht belonging to Mavic Chen.

Bret, more determined than ever to get to Earth to warn the authorities that Chen is a traitor (he has Marc Cory's tape), has to work with Steven on some rapid repairs to the space vessel when it is forced down onto the prison planet Desperus.

But on the flight from Desperus, Katarina sacrifices her life in order to save the other three from the evil intentions of a psychopathic multi-killer, Kirksen.

Once on Earth they find they are not safe. Fellow Space Security agent Sara Kingdom shoots Bret down before the Doctor and Steven can convince her that Vyon was no traitor – as Chen had told her. By this time it is already too late to do anything about Mavic Chen, as the three are accidentally transported to the world of Mira by cellular projection.

Attacked by the invisible Visians, they are forced to escape from an invading troop of Daleks in the Daleks' own vessel. Here the Doctor uses the on-board laboratory to make a non-functioning facsimile of the Tarranium Core. The Dalek ship is programmed to return to Kembel in spite of all their efforts to divert it, and it falls to Steven to hand over the fake core to the Daleks once the Doctor and Sara are aboard the TARDIS.

On their travels again they find, after a brief interlude for Christmas, that they are being followed. They land on the volcanic planet of Tigus only to discover it is not the Daleks but their old foe from 1066, the Time Meddling Monk. His first plan of revenge fails but he follows them to ancient Egypt, where they are joined by the Daleks and Mavic Chen, who know their Core was a fake. With much difficulty the Doctor and his party escape, but only after surrendering the real core. However the Doctor has taken the directional unit from the Monk's TARDIS and with it they get back to Kembel, knowing that only by returning there have they any chance of thwarting the Daleks.

The Daleks have double-crossed the outer galaxies and after the Doctor rescues them, their representatives leave to warn the Universe of the dangers of Dalek ambitions. Mavic Chen captures Steven and Sara. He still believes that only through the Daleks can he achieve supreme power. In return, the Daleks execute him.

The Doctor manages to steal and activate the Time Destructor, but although the Dalek invasion force is wiped out Sara ages to death before his eyes, and he is only just rescued by Steven. Almost drained of energy the two of them leave Kembel, once a jungle world, now just dust and sand.

**Background:** Never before or since equalled for its length, number of sets and sheer volume of visual effects, this twelve part story remains a testament to the skills, planning and resourcefulness of *Doctor Who*'s most formative Director, Douglas Camfield, now sadly deceased.

Motivation for this monumental serial, so the story goes, hailed from Programme Head Huw Weldon who suggested to Verity Lambert and Dennis Spooner a mammoth-length Dalek production because, allegedly, his mother was a great fan of the Daleks. Spooner picked up on this idea and thought the best way to do it would be as an extended *Perils of Pauline*-type adventure, complete with 'How are they going to get out of that?' endings.

Neither Spooner nor Nation felt able to handle the writing task singly, so they chose to split the work half and half, with Spooner

Mavic Chen's spacecraft, *The Spar*. An electric motor operated the revolving aeriel and the ship was flown on thin nylon wires.

OVERLEAF:
Shooting the model scenes on the twenty foot square table-top set of the Daleks' landing pad.

acting as unofficial Script Editor for the production. The initial storyline came from Terry Nation, but as an amusement for themselves the two writers took it in turns to write the detailed story breakdowns, each leaving an impossible cliff-hanger which the other writer had to get out of.

Although nominally Producer and Script Editor for the series, neither John Wiles nor Donald Tosh had much to do with this serial, the former greatly resenting it as a three-month obstacle to his attempts to raise *Doctor Who* towards a more sophisticated and adult level.

So great were the production demands on this story that both Barry Newbery and Ramond Cusick were pulled in to design its visual composition. Broadly speaking, Cusick handled the early space opera episodes while Newbery tackled the later time-travel instalments.

Special effects for this show were highly inventive, achieving on a shoestring budget a look comparable with many much more expensive feature films. Needing footage of the Visians briefly becoming visible when fired at by the Daleks, Camfield shot on film an actor writhing in a white sack against a black background. Muzzily overlaying this film onto recorded shots of the Daleks firing into the jungle – complete with 'negative' effect – gave an image similar in impact to the Id monster fight featured in the classic sf film *Forbidden Planet*.

Other optical effects, such as the montaged graphics sequence showing the Doctor, Sara and Bret being 'matter transported' to Mira helped inspire the Effects Designers working on the stargate sequences for Kubrick's *2001: A Space Odyssey*.

In casting too Camfield was fortunate, landing Jean Marsh, Nicholas Courtney, Peter Butterworth and Kevin Stoney as guest stars, the latter winning the *Daily Express* 1965 reader's poll for *Best TV Villain of the Year*.

Only in one area did he fail. For the special Christmas episode, 'The Feast of Steven', an episode never screened abroad, Camfield wanted to use the main actors and sets from the popular *Z Cars* series (including Brian Blessed, Colin Welland and James Ellis) in cameo appearances. The word from *Z Cars* Producer David Rose, fearing a send-up of a publicly respected programme, was a very firm 'No' . . .

## Production Credits

Serial 'V'
Twelve Episodes
Black and White

| | |
|---|---|
| 'The Nightmare Begins' | 13 November 1965 |
| 'Day of Armageddon' | 20 November 1965 |
| 'Devil's Planet' | 27 November 1965 |
| 'The Traitors' | 4 December 1965 |
| 'Counter-Plot' | 11 December 1965 |
| 'Coronas of the Sun' | 18 December 1965 |
| 'The Feast of Steven' | 25 December 1965 |
| 'Volcano' | 1 January 1966 |
| 'Golden Death' | 8 January 1966 |
| 'Escape Switch' | 15 January 1966 |
| 'The Abandoned Planet' | 22 January 1966 |
| 'Destruction of Time' | 29 January 1966 |

### Cast

| | |
|---|---|
| Doctor Who | William Hartnell |
| Steven | Peter Purves |
| Katarina | Adrienne Hill |
| Sara Kingdom | Jean Marsh |
| Bret Vyon | Nicholas Courtney |
| Mavic Chen | Kevin Stoney |
| Kert Gantry | Brian Cant |
| Lizan | Pamela Greer |
| Roald | Philip Anthony |
| Interviewer | Michael Guest |
| Dalek Voices | Peter Hawkins, David Graham |
| Daleks | Kevin Manser, Robert Jewell, Gerald Taylor, John Scott-Martin |
| Technix | Hugh Cecil, Gary Peller, John Cam, David Freed, Dennis Tate, Ashley Bowring |
| Zephon | Julian Sherrier |
| Trantis | Roy Evans |
| Kirksen | Douglas Sheldon |
| Bors | Dallas Cavell |
| Garge | Geoffrey Cheshire |
| Criminals | Beatrice Greetz, Jack Le White, Rene Heath, M. J. Matthews |
| Karlton | Maurice Browning |
| Daxtar | Roger Avon |
| Borkar | James Hall |
| Froyn | Bill Meilen |
| Rhynmal | John Herrington |
| Visian | Francis Whilley |
| The Meddling Monk | Peter Butterworth |
| Station Sergeant | Clifford Earl |
| First Policeman | Norman Mitchell |
| Second Policeman | Malcolm Rogers |

193

| | |
|---|---|
| Detective-Inspector | Kenneth Thornett |
| Man in Mackintosh | Reg Pritchard |
| Blossom Lefavre | Sheila Dunn |
| Darcy Tranton | Leonard Grahame |
| Steinberger P. Green | Royston Tickner |
| Ingmar Knopf | Mark Ross |
| Assistant Director | Conrad Monk |
| Arab Sheik | David James |
| Vamp | Paula Topham |
| Clown | Robert G. Jewell |
| Professor Webster | Albert Barrington |
| Prop Man | Buddy Windrush |
| Cameraman | Steve Machin |
| First Keystone Cop | Paul Sarony |
| Second Keystone Cop | Malcolm Leopold |
| Ingmar Knopf's Cameraman | Jack Le White |
| Make-up Man | Harry Davies |
| Cowboy | William Hall |
| Saloon Bar Girl | Jean Pastell |
| Chaplin | M. J. Matthews |
| Celation | Terence Woodfield |
| Gearon | Jack Pitt |
| Trevor | Roger Brierley |
| Scott | Bruce Wightman |
| Khepren | Jeffrey Isaac |
| Tuthmos | Derek Ware |
| Hyksos | Walter Randall |
| Malpha | Bryan Mosley |
| Beaus | Gerry Videl |
| Old Sara | May Warden |
| Egyptian Warriors and Slaves | Terry Leigh, Valentino Musetti, Agit Chauhan, Bruno Castagnoli, David Shaurat, John Caesar, Clay Hunter, Anthony Lang, Peter Johnson, Len Russell, Ray Mirioni, Ali Hassan, Paul Philips, Faul Bahadour, Andrew Andreas, Clenn Whitter |
| Extras | John Cam, Dennis Tate, Ian East, Brian Edwards, Gerry Videl, David Freed |

**Crew**

| | |
|---|---|
| Production Assistants | Victors Ritelis, Michael Briant |
| Assistant Floor Managers | Catherine Childs, Caroline Walmsley |
| Costume Supervisor | Daphne Dare |
| Make-up Supervisor | Sonia Markham |
| Music | Tristram Cary |
| Designers | Raymond Cusick (1–2, 5–7, 11) |
| | Barry Newbery (3–4, 8–10, 12) |
| Producer | John Wiles |
| Director | Douglas Camfield |

# THE BRIDE OF SACRIFICE

IN 1963 ABC TV published the findings of an experiment they had conducted some time earlier into the perception thresholds of children watching Television. Overseers of the experiment included Mary Field, ABC's Consultant on Children's Programmes, Professor Arnold Lloyd of Cambridge University's Education Department, and Sydney Newman, then still Drama Supervisor at ABC.

The experiment involved secretly filming a group of children, ranged in age groups of ten to thirteen, watching a never-before-seen episode of a science fiction serial. The researchers were already aware that choice of subject matter determined much of the degree of interest shown in any programme. What they wanted to know was the form and composition of that interest, and how the presentation of the subject matter helped or hindered it. The spectrum of questions for which answers were sought took in everything from specifics, like 'Are dialogue sequences less compelling than action scenes?' to abstracts querying the very suspension of disbelief principle thought essential to any form of drama viewing – especially children's viewing.

The programme selected for this experiment was an episode of *Pathfinders to Venus*, a series already demonstrated as the main forerunner of *Doctor Who*. Studying the reactions of the groups watching the episode, and questioning some of the children afterwards about what they had seen, Mary Field and *Pathfinders* Director Guy Verney felt re-affirmed in their beliefs about the value of the six clear principles governing drama television production. These six principles, which appeared from the experiment to relate as much to children as to adults, were:

The need for good plot, clearly developed.

The need for crisp, pregnant dialogue.

The need for convincing acting.

The need to avoid irrelevant action.

The need for careful presentation of dramatic points.

The need for a rhythmic relaxation of tension.

The comments by Field and Verney concluded with a strong recommendation that every resource of television production should be lavished on programmes for children 'if they are to watch intelligently and develop into ready viewers for that "better" Television being demanded by the critics' and sought after by the industry itself.

Architect of the drive towards 'People's Television', Sydney Newman took with him to the BBC his observations on the experiment, which he summed up by saying, 'Children of today, who make up part of our vast audience, are well informed and are capable of some pretty sophisticated judgements. As ten-year-olds, as long as our plays are exciting and clear, they'll play along with us and watch. If we lose them as doubting teenagers by not stimulating them with well-made and provocative stories, what kind of audiences will we have left when they become adults?'

The devising of the four central characters for *Doctor Who* was intended to embody the essence of the above observations. On the shoulders of these characters would rest a final responsibility for conveying four of the six principles of TV drama out to the audiences at home. In an era still almost a decade from the feasibility of spectacle and complex visual effects as substitutes for performance, the actors were the be-all and end-all of dramatic presentation.

Thus, on her appointment as Producer, Verity Lambert had to give careful consideration to the casting of her four main leads. The whole format of *Doctor Who* evoked the feeling of a tiny, close-knit group constantly under threat from whatever menace lay beyond the sanctuary of the TARDIS. Other characters would come into the show, but for never longer than seven weeks, thereby strengthening the viewer's identification with, and reliance on, the reactions of the regulars to these guest characters and novel situations.

Carole Ann Ford, who played Susan, the Doctor's granddaughter, as she is today.

196

The casting of an actress to play Susan was the most problematic of the three companion characters. For Ian Chesterton a robust, slightly heroic actor was quickly found in William Russell, widely remembered for his title role in the ITV film series *Sir Lancelot*. Similarly, Jacqueline Hill was a strong contender for the part of Barbara from the very start, thanks to her critically acclaimed part in the TV play *Six Proud Walkers*.

The part of Susan, though, went through a lot of casting before Verity Lambert arrived at Carole Ann Ford, including the auditioning of juvenile actress Jackie Lane, who eventually landed the part of Dodo Chaplet some years later. Part of the problem was an initial doubt about the type of actress the Production team wanted, as Carole Ann Ford explains:

'There are some types of actress who are employed because they have a specific personality useful for one type of performance. So that, no matter what they do, they are more or less giving the same performance each time. A Director will cast this type of actress because he knows that is the kind of personality he wants brought out in this character, and he can rely on that actress to give just such a performance.

'On the other hand, if you're a character actress you're allowed much more freedom to question the role you've been given, and to go more deeply into it to find a means of playing the part. In other words, there are certain roles which are tailor-made for certain people who will go along and just be more or less themselves, and other roles which do require a lot of – if you like – psychoanalysis beforehand to get the most out of the part.'

Carole Ann Ford made her first film appearance at the age of eight, retired to school for a few years, and then emerged again at fifteen, working constantly thereafter until her landing of the part of Susan Foreman in the Summer of 1963.

'I very much wanted to be a character actress, to be able to lose myself in various parts. I'd have been very happy playing an old lady of ninety at the age of fifteen. For me, the whole point of acting is using different aspects of yourself, and getting as far away from yourself as you can. I think you find most actors and actresses agree that the hardest thing sometimes is just to be yourself, because most people just don't know who they really are.

'I never went to any formal acting school – in fact, I've probably just been very, very lucky getting all the parts I have – though for as long as I can remember all I ever wanted to be was an actress, and to be in the Theatre.'

Carole Ann Ford is very proud that, up to her casting for *Doctor Who*, she never played the same type of role twice. She was a French Resistance girl in the series *Moonstrike*, a ballet dancer in a spy thriller, a nurse in *Emergency Ward Ten*, a secretary in *Compact*, and in the film *Mix Me A Person* she played Adam Faith's girlfriend. If any one common factor did stand out it was her tendency to play parts older than herself.

Strangely, it was the part of a girl in her mid-twenties (close to Carole Ann Ford's own age at the time), in the traumatic play *Man on a Bicycle*, that won her an invitation to visit the *Doctor Who*

198

Office and discuss the role of Susan with Verity Lambert. Lambert and Director Waris Hussein had been present in the gallery during the recording of *Man on a Bicycle* and were impressed by Carole Ann Ford's ability to scream and behave hysterically, ie: to act a very trauma-ridden part convincingly. Although most of *Doctor Who*'s scripts, at this time, were still in a fairly fluid state, the nature of the show – populated with murderous warlords, malevolent Daleks, or savage cavemen – called for a character capable of conveying terror to the audience. Because of the intention still to present Ian and Barbara as calm, balanced individuals, this attribute was thought best foisted on the teenage character.

As to how Susan would be played when not required to scream, the initial sales pitch was glowing in the extreme:

'Oh, what she wasn't going to be! First of all, she was going to be hyper-hyper-intelligent. She was going to have a telepathic communication with her grandfather. She was going to have every physical attribute you could possibly imagine: a kind of step-up from the *Avengers* Honor Blackman lady – doing all sorts of physical stunts, judo and karate. *And* she was going to have wonderful costumes, specifically designed for her, featured in each story.

'I do remember, at the discussions with Verity, they even had a few sketches done of the kind of clothes she would wear. We spent some time going through a whole heap of magazines with a girl from the Costume Department, picking out a design here and there and saying, "Yes, that sort of thing would be a good idea for her, wouldn't it?" Then I asked, as we were going to go from century to century, if I could be allowed to collect a few bits of paraphernalia as we went along – odd little items that had taken my fancy which would then turn up in other stories. Again they said yes, that seemed like a good idea, great, marvellous. So what happened in the end? It was all scrapped!

'A little bit of it was brought into the very first episode, the pilot, where I was allowed to play her slightly weird. I was allowed to give the impression that there was a helluva lot more going on behind her façade, but again that was taken out when we came to do the episode again for the version seen on Television.'

While *Doctor Who*'s master minds shied away from narrative innovations – possibly fearful of losing standardised character identification tags, useful in cementing an audience's interest – appearance-wise Susan was permitted to have a somewhat startling appearance.

Summer 1963 saw England still a year away from its pop culture explosion which so changed fashions, music, ideas and outlooks for years to come. Even the Beatles were only just a national phenomenon, although interest had widened outward from their music to include their somewhat innovative hair styles. With an eye for contemporary styling Verity Lambert agreed that Susan Foreman should have specially-cut hair, radically different from the back-combed, upswept or pony-tail styles of her early Sixties class mates.

OVERLEAF:
Susan, Barbara, Ian and the Doctor confront the Sensorites.

199

'I had very long hair when Verity and the others first saw me, down below my shoulders, very thick and very curly. They decided they wanted to make me look unusual, to make me look "spacey", and so they cut it all off.'

The haircut, however, evolved into far more than just a one-off for a TV series. Allowed to choose her hairdresser, Carole Ann Ford plumped for an up-and-coming young stylist she had known and visited for some time named Vidal Sassoon.

'We never got any recognition for it, but Vidal's short, geometric look, which made his name and got him into the news, had never before been seen. He designed that look for Susan Foreman, and indeed arranged to open his shop specially for me one evening so I could be ready for the production day next morning.

'Ironically by the time we came to do the first episode again, my hair had grown a little longer, so it wasn't quite as eye-catching, but even so I think it's a very unrecognised feather in *Doctor Who*'s cap that we created the look which launched Vidal Sassoon on his road to fame and fortune.'

A great many 'What if?' questions could be asked on the balance the Production Office achieved in its casting of William Hartnell, Jacqueline Hill, William Russell and Carole Ann Ford to play the four regulars. What if Jacqueline Hill had not been available? Would another actress have fitted so perfectly the pensive, slightly sad role she created that so encapsulated Sydney Newman's wish for human characters in awe of their out-of-time surroundings? Very probably the strong, stable presences of Ian and Barbara did much to wean the Production teams off the idea of making Susan into a high-kicking, karate-chopping supergirl as seen in ITV's *The Avengers*. Either *Doctor Who* would be drama, or it would be adventure. And drama won.

Coming onto a new series for the first time could be a daunting prospect even to the acting profession's hardy perennials. Always at the back of the mind are worries over how well one will get on with the other artists. The outset of *Doctor Who* multiplied those worries fourfold, in that each of the regular cast was (a) unused to science fiction; (b) unused to each other; and (c) stuck with a year's contract to do the part, like it or not. Fortunately the working environment on the show, from the cast's point of view, gelled very quickly almost from Day One.

'We all thought we were going to hate each other. We had a photo session at somewhere like a hotel – it wasn't one of the studios – and I remember looking at Jackie [Hill] and thinking, "Ooh, she looks a bit formidable." You see, what I didn't know, is that she was feeling terribly nervous as well, just as I was. She was looking very severe with a sort of no-nonsense look about her, and I began thinking, "Oh no, it doesn't look like we're going to be friends." But then, luckily, I met Bill Russell who was very sweet and I thought, "Well maybe . . ." And then finally I got introduced to Bill Hartnell, and that really broke the ice. From then on we became the best of friends, to the extent that I can't remember us having even one argument.'

202

That the four lead artists got on so well with each other was a distinct advantage in coping with the pressurised working schedules they were expected to maintain over the next year. For a greater majority of the time the supposed glamour of Television was an entirely invisible commodity.

The working week began every Monday, rain or shine. On Monday, each of the cast, regular and story-contracted, would make their way, under their own steam (no chauffeured limousines here) to a pre-designated rehearsal room. Sometimes this would be a church hall, sometimes a Territorial Army drill hall, occasionally even a London Transport recreation room. The common linking factor was a close proximity to Shepherds Bush Green, home of the Production Office. Very often, uncommon denominators were the premises' rainproofing . . .

'Forget all you read about the glamour of Television. One of the places we used was in such a state of unrepair that every time it rained we had to put out buckets everywhere just to keep our feet dry.'

The purpose of the Monday morning assembly was to meet the Director of the week, his team of assistants, and to read through the script of the episode due to be recorded that Friday. Script Editor David Whitaker would be on hand in case any of the script 'didn't work', needed padding, needed shortening, even, on one occasion, needed a total rewrite to make it 'workable'. Sometimes too, Verity Lambert and Mervyn Pinfield would be present.

By lunchtime it was expected that the sit-down run throughs would be complete and timed to run an optimum length of twenty-four minutes, thirty seconds. That would leave the afternoon free for the first walk-around rehearsals where the Director would begin working out his cast, camera and microphone boom movements. For the artists this day would be their first sight of the script due in production on Friday. But if all had gone well, the creative team of Designers, Make-up and Costume Supervisors would already have been briefed on their requirements from the script days ago. The Designer's floor model and plans would be complete with set construction hopefully under way. Measurements would have been taken from the guest cast enabling the Costume Supervisor either to begin tailoring any special costumes (a Sensorite uniform for instance), or to arrange hiring of costumes from BBC stock or from Theatrical Costumiers such as Bermans & Nathans – who had supplied William Hartnell's Edwardian outfit as the Doctor.

That was the ideal. Very often there were problems getting everything done to time, and especially on the first season, availability of scripts for Monday morning was the cause of many a delay.

'I'm not joking, we literally, sometimes, used to sit there round a big table waiting for the scripts to come in. We might be given the first few pages to be going on with, and as we went along more pages would arrive. Then we'd usually have to change them like mad. During the read-through we'd all be busy with our little pencils, marking out sections of dialogue, and saying at the end,

"Don't you think we should change this to read like that? What do you think?" It's the only time there were ever arguments over scripts, but they had to be said.

'We all got to know our characters as the weeks went by. We developed an understanding of what they thought, what they felt, and how they behaved towards each other. Occasionally you'd get a script come down with lines in it you instinctively knew your character just wouldn't say, or actions she just wouldn't do, particularly from writers who were new to the show. So then you had to argue it out to get the script changed to how it ought to read.'

More often than not script changes were brought in line with the regular artist's ease of reading the part, because of the burden placed on them. By the time of the camera rehearsals at Lime Grove on Friday morning, the day of recording, everyone was expected to be word perfect, with the equivalent of a twenty-five minute play committed firmly to memory. The dictates of continuous recording precluded the luxury afforded actors in the Film Industry – who could learn a few lines, act out one scene, rest, learn a few more lines, and so on. In Television, at this time, line discipline was as rigid as for twice-nightly, weekly rep in the Theatre. One saving grace was that television drama preferred scenes of short, crisp dialogue which artists, by and large, preferred to doing large chunks of monologue or narration more common in the Theatre. This form of dramatic presentation was the key to Carole Ann Ford's own learning technique.

'It's much easier if you can mentally align movement with lines. You think to yourself, when I move from there to there I say whatever, and then when I move back to here I say the following. And you can widen it to take in other people's lines and movements so they act as springboards for you. This is why it does throw you quite a lot if another actor forgets his move, because it churns up in your brain the sequences you've worked out and are expecting.'

As the eldest and most senior member of the regular troupe William Hartnell was frequently the cause of many a recording break due to memory lapses occasionally so hilarious as to cause Directors and artists alike to question their accidence. Some of these 'Hartnellisms' have since passed into lexical history . . .

'I'm not sure if it was "The Reign of Terror" story about the French Revolution, or one of the other ones, but we had a terrible time getting Bill to pronounce the word brazier, meaning a rack for burning coals. Each time he'd get to the line about going to stoke the brazier it would come out as "stoke the brassière", which of course stopped everything dead and brought the Director screaming down on us. To this day I was never sure whether Bill used to do these kind of things accidentally or on purpose.'

The frenetic pace established to get an episode 'into the can' each Friday certainly left very little time for breaking tension even with the odd unscheduled moment of humorous diversion. If things did go wrong, especially during recording, it was counted a major disaster, increasing proportionately in scale the nearer to

10.00 pm the clock ticked.

One episode with disasters aplenty was Episode Four of 'The Keys of Marinus', the episode set in the polar regions of that planet. In a bid to simulate a cave of ice the set walls were coated in a fibre-glass matte mixture which gave them a shiny, brittle look under the correct lighting. Unfortunately, not only did the surface become very brittle it also became razor sharp, giving rise to numerous complaints of cuts and scrapes from actors during rehearsal. Then, mid-way through live recording, the bridge collapsed . . .

The bridge in question was a rope bridge strung, *Indiana Jones*-style, between two cliff ledges, although thankfully a lot nearer the ground than its later film equivalent. Carole Ann Ford had just begun a crossing from one side to the other when, without warning, the supports gave way, pitching her over and down to a very rough landing at the foot of 'the cliff'. Luckily no-one was injured and recording recommenced once the bridge had been resecured. However, as Carole Ann Ford pointed out, anyone viewing the episode with hindsight can easily spot signs of great anxiety among several of the cast required to cross that gaping ravine.

For its distinct absence of bridges, cave sets and other hazards, Carole Ann Ford's favourite story remained the two part adventure set entirely within the TARDIS 'The Edge of Destruction'. For her it was one of the few instances where Susan was allowed to be anything other than a 15-year-old schoolgirl. Her favourite scene was the sequence of Susan, partially concussed, menacing Ian with the points of a long pair of scissors, threatening to stab him until she gives in and vents her rage instead on the mattress of her bed. Powerful material for 1963 but a sample of how the show should have developed its characters to make them more rounded and believable. As things transpired, however:

'We tried desperately to get out of the format of landing somewhere, splitting up, getting lost and getting captured, getting into trouble and getting out of it. We tried to make suggestions for character developments, all of which they wouldn't allow.

'They wouldn't allow me to grow up. I was fifteen and that was that. I was stuck with that age even though at least a year had gone by. I remember I suggested it might be fun if Susan developed a crush on Ian, but they wouldn't allow that either. I suppose the reason was one of policy really – they had the youngsters hooked and they wanted to keep them in that position by not rocking the boat. Part of the problem was that I was only in my twenties when I did it, and therefore still quite young in their eyes. I didn't have a big name in the business as I'd been concentrating just on working, so I wasn't a star and couldn't force through any changes.

'Bill [Hartnell] tried for me. Bill agreed with me that Susan should be more interesting. I used to go to him and say, "Bill, please try and get them to do this", and he did fight for me quite a lot, but it was an uphill struggle all the way. I don't think they knew how to write for me as they did for Jackie and Russ [William Russell]. And in a way I lost my direction too when all my lovely ideas about what I hoped to do were smashed down, leaving only a shell: a two-dimensional character instead of a many-faceted character, which would have been more interesting to watch and more interesting to do.

'I think it was quite a victory, looking at 'The Aztecs', that they allowed me some leeway there: having me chosen as the wife of the Warrior, which more or less said, look she's marriageable now. The two-parter was also fun as it gave all of us a chance to act in conflict and be a bit more expansive, because otherwise, if you think about it, all we were doing most of the time was feeding lines to other people.'

Some of the limitations placed on the cast stemmed directly from the immediate and mass popularity *Doctor Who* enjoyed almost from its first week on air. Most television drama attracts some mail from interested viewers but rarely does that mail arrive by the sackful. By the end of 'The Daleks' the *Doctor Who* office was regularly receiving a sackful of mail per day, sometimes two sackfuls. A staggering quantity of it related to the Daleks, most of which was farmed out to Terry Nation or Raymond Cusick, but the four main characters got their share as well. Initially flattering for the recognition it brought, the vast and continuous bundles of fan request mail eventually proved intrusive to the artists' private lives as their characters entered public domain.

'We all got very tired towards the end of the year. *Doctor Who* got so incredibly popular that you found your weekends were no longer free either. Those got taken up with a lot of promotional work, and in my case I found that charities got in touch with me a lot to open fêtes, attend jumble sales, etc. Eventually I thought the only way I could control what I was doing was to decide on one specific charity – I chose Muscular Dystrophy – and work just with them, which is what I did.

'The public's reaction to *Doctor Who* was extraordinary. The type of fans the show attracted was so widespread. It wasn't just kids. One would literally get letters from eight to eighty, with a tremendous number of university students, all asking questions about the motivation of the series, how long it was going to carry on, questions I wasn't even qualified to answer sometimes.

'Then there was the Press. The Press went mad on *Doctor Who*. On the few occasions I did get some time off to go somewhere, there would be photographers everywhere, besieging me at the airport as if I was some international film star going to Hollywood. It really was extraordinary.'

The standard contracts the four regulars signed bound them to the show for its estimated minimum run of one production year. On the BBC's side they retained a further option to wind up any contract after eight weeks if they elected to replace an artist, or if the show was cancelled. *Doctor Who*'s success ensured no exercising of either of the BBC's options, but for the regular actors and actresses it meant there was no escape until the end of Year One. By mid-1964 Carole Ann Ford was the only member of the cast anxious to leave, resigned to the fact that the Production Office were uninterested in expanding her role beyond that of a line-feed, and wary of the prospect of being typecast forever as a 'kooky, fifteen-year-old science fiction' girl.

Carole Ann Ford's departure at the end of 'The Dalek Invasion of Earth' saw just such fears realised. Offers duly came in, but always to play an extension of Susan Foreman. Television Producers would not cast her in lead roles, knowing full well the public would immediately identify her as 'that *Doctor Who* girl'. So after *Doctor Who* Carole Ann Ford deliberately immersed herself in theatrical parts to free herself from the stigma of Television, emerging only after a year to play the radically different role of a prostitute in ITV's new *Public Eye* series.

Nevertheless, her year with *Doctor Who* left Carole Ann Ford with many fond memories of the people both behind and in front of the cameras.

'A lot of people I've spoken to ask me about Bill [Hartnell] as though he was some sort of monster. In actual fact he was a very vulnerable guy, a very kind guy, but like a lot of people who are vulnerable and sensitive he tended to put up a front to disguise it. Only if you got beneath this front would you find out what a gentle and caring man he was. But you had to get past that first because Bill was always frightened of somebody, perhaps, trying to get the better of him. He was a good actor, and this front was an acted part he'd assume to get his own way.

'Verity was always very approachable. She was very young, very much one of us, very friendly, very open to suggestions, but very strong about the limitations too. She was always so in control about everything which is what gave her this air of being much older than just twenty-seven. You always knew when she was annoyed, because she went icy cool and would smile a lot, rather like all the best gangsters do in films – a frightening dichotomy.

'David Whitaker was always a very sweet man, very jokey about everything, while Mervyn was always so fussy. He was forever correcting people about pronunciations and points of grammar – very pedantic about how things should be said and done.'

But crowning all Carole Ann Ford's reminiscences are the classic 'Hartnellisms' that did so much to inject notes of levity into a very hard working production cycle.

'We had a device aboard the TARDIS called the Fault Locator which we ran over and examined every time anything went wrong with the ship. Part way through this episode something was due to malfunction on the console and the Doctor would say something like, "Quick, Susan, go and check the Fault Locator." Well, this bit came up, the lights started flashing, big panic, and the Doctor turns to me and says, "Quick, Susan, go and check the Fornicator . . ."'

# THE FINAL TEST

How DOES a programme get judged? How do Directors, Producers, Department Heads, even whole companies and corporations find out whether the programmes they have made are compelling viewing, averagely popular, or instant cures for insomnia?

This problem was first addressed by the BBC as far back as the early days of radio. With newspapers, periodicals and books, assessment was easy. If a paper was popular, it sold and money accrued accordingly. The more popular the paper, the more copies it sold, producing direct one-to-one ratios with the balance sheets. Broadcasting was different. Licence revenue could only tell how many receivers had been sold the length and breadth of the UK. It could not tell when those receivers were switched on, nor what programmes were being heard.

The solution was the tried and tested market research technique of sampling. Each week teams of representatives, either from the BBC or from some independently commissioned research body, would knock on the doors of several hundred 'average houses' (the

209

selection of 'average houses' being an art in itself) and quiz their occupants on which programmes had been listened to, how many in the house had heard them, the age groups of those listening, and reactions to those programmes.

With some refinements, this process carried over into Television after the war, the results becoming more vital to the broadcasting powers with the arrival of ITV in the 1950s. As competition between the Corporation and the Network hotted up, so too did the need to manufacture widely popular programmes.

The Daleks made *Doctor Who* a key audience-grabbing programme. Their success in attracting up to eight million viewers early in the evening made the show a vanguard in the BBC's bid to seize the lion's share of the audience for the peak night of the week, which was Saturday. Correspondingly, the BBC studied very carefully any feedback they received concerning the show.

Along with audience research, much of this in the early years came from the newspapers, many of which would not let a week go by without some comment on the programme.

Predictably much of the press reaction centred around the Daleks, evaluations of which confirmed the widely-held internal belief at the BBC that *Doctor Who* was achieving audiences 'under six and over sixty'. However, as some commentators pointed out, not always was this being done by the conventional route.

'I don't think *Doctor Who* is a children's programme at all. It is an adults' programme addressed to adults via children. Many

OVERLEAF:
The Doctor on the trail of the
Savages. Despite the story's
intelligent script, ratings for
'The Savages' were low,
reflecting a general
disillusionment with the TV
series at that time.

stories – *Alice*, *Gulliver's Travels*, *The Wind in the Willows* – are like that,' commented Brian Jackson, Director of the Advisory Centre for Education. Turning specifically to one of the Dalek serials, Mr Jackson went on to say, 'With its undefined echoes of Hiroshima, concentration camps, and Kafkaesque corridors it was very much out of the stuff of our time.'

Ann Purser, a mother of three reviewing for *The Daily Telegraph*, summed up very succinctly the reaction of most children to Terry Nation's immortal machines. 'I remember being asked some time ago by an earnest lady who was putting the Daleks on stage for a Christmas show, "What are your children's reactions to the Daleks? We think they should be more frightening." I had to admit that one child curled up with laughter, one shook with terror and the other, being one-year-old, couldn't stick it long enough to produce any positive reaction.'

Generally, critics were in favour of the way in which Daleks enthralled their young audiences, but wary of some of the ideas presented to children by these robots. A writer for *The Guardian* reported a father as being 'disturbed' by the notion of his infant child retiring to bed with the word 'Exterminate' on her mind, but he added, 'He had watched Saturday's episode with his daughter, his son, aged five, and two other children of the same age. They were enthralled from beginning to end, and ever since have been

211

Vicki and Koquillion from 'The Rescue', the only story the regular cast all refused to do at first.

playing Daleks. Yesterday, though, the same group had watched Dumas' *The Three Musketeers* and this had proved far more disturbing.'

By 1966 the novelty of the Daleks' initial appearance had worn off, leaving observers, both within and outside the BBC, undecided as to their continued pulling power. Again in *The Guardian*, Mr John Bennett, a member of the committee of the Society for Education in Film and Television, expressed the opinion that the Daleks were losing their power now that much of the mystery surrounding them had been cleared up. Nevertheless, he went on to add, 'Most children have a sinking fear of Daleks, especially at the age of seven or eight. They are frightened because these Daleks are without a personality they can understand. Daleks, after all, kill willy-nilly, and that is all they live for.'

In all, Dalek stories comprised some thirty-two episodes out of William Hartnell's grand total of 134, a fair representation, but

still with the greater bulk of material relying on other 'hooks' for the programme's fascination. Assessing these stories required far greater reliance on the BBC's own audience research sampling system.

Distributing questionnaires among volunteer viewing panels, the BBC graded the appreciation percentage results into five categories: A+, A, B, C and C−, with A+ expressing the 'wouldn't have missed it for the world' opinion, and C− the 'complete waste of time' reaction.

The report for 'The Romans' broke down into the following:

| A+ | A | B | C | C− |
|----|-----|-----|-----|-----|
| 7% | 26% | 37% | 20% | 10% |

which, in turn, was gauged to be seven points down on the second season of *Doctor Who*'s average Audience Reaction Index.

The questionnaires also gave room for comments from the panelists, many of whom expressed the generally held views about the historicals which gradually, throughout 1965 and 1966, steered the Producers of the series away from stories set in Earth's past, and hence away from Sydney Newman's ideal of the show as an educational experience.

'This programme gets more and more bizarre; in fact it's so ridiculous it's a bore,' declared one of a number of viewers reporting, who apparently agreed that *Doctor Who* was 'only suitable for morons'. Indeed the conclusion of the adventure in Ancient Rome, though not always provoking such stringent condemnation, found the majority of the sample audience in carping mood. It was evident that the sequence had often been a disappointment – some viewers alleged that, after a promising start, the story had steadily declined to a farcical and pathetic anti-climax, while others were 'not keen on *Doctor Who* going historical', preferring the futuristic tales and the element of horror provided by weird creatures on 'non-existent planets' – a taste which some claimed was shared by their children ('they enjoy a fright now and again' and 'the more monsters the better'). On the other hand, there were complaints (though fewer) that there had been too much violence in this sequence, and that it was unsuitable for children. A fairly common criticism, however, was its lack of realism – everything, it was said, was 'transparently phoney'.

To do 'The Romans' as a comedy had been Verity Lambert's idea as a means of injecting a livelier sparkle into the historicals. 'Marco Polo', arguably, had the best script of all the Hartnell shows, but public reaction had indicated a wish for more action in place of lyrical stylising. The substitution of comedy plus action should have remedied the apparent downbeat responses to the historicals, but it didn't. About the only aspect of 'The Romans' to win universal acclaim was the high acting standard Christopher Barry coached from his cast:

'Others acknowledged their efforts in coping with material which gave them few opportunities; and a small majority of partisans were quite satisfied with a good all-round performance, in which Derek Francis had apparently supplied a striking cameo

PREVIOUS PAGE:
The Doctor is 'escorted' by Captain Edal's guards to the city of the Elders in this scene from 'The Savages'.

218

of Nero, and William Hartnell had outshone all the rest in the principal role.'

Strong words and very suggestive that the basic faults with the story lay with its script and the whole general notion of continuing to present historical adventures in a series clearly loved by the public for its science fiction content.

Scripting was an area under continual analysis by members of *Doctor Who*'s production team, encouraged, no doubt, by Sydney Newman's drive towards plain-statement drama. Christopher Barry in particular, a former member of Ealing Studios' script department, added a lot of input and comment to the narrative process, shown here by a letter he sent to Verity Lambert on reading through the first draft script of 'The Rescue' – the only story the entire regular cast refused to do at first:

'The chief overall fault of this serial appears to be that Koquillion's behaviour and the reasons for it are not consistent, neither are they sufficiently menacing.

'Bennett/Koquillion is a pathological case, a schizoid in whom each half knows about the other side of his character. He is deliberate in everything he does, and it all has a mad kind of logic. Although, were he a human on our Earth we might feel pity for him, we must feel none for him here.

'He has killed (so he thinks) everyone on the planet except Tanni [Vicki] and he wants to kill Doctor Who and his companions so his secret is kept. (Just why he doesn't kill Tanni, we don't seem to know: I imagine for sexual motives . . .) Everything he does in this story must spring from his desire to kill and at no time must he allow any of them to escape as he does at present. It is this weakness in Koquillion as a character that gives rise to other weaknesses in the script. Put this right and I think the rest will follow. Because Koquillion's menace is not channelled towards our heroes they seem to do things arbitrarily to suit the dictates of the script and not for any real purpose.'

The fate of the historical adventures was finally decided by Producer Innes Lloyd, who formally succeeded John Wiles as from 'The Celestial Toymaker'. Under his scrutiny the whole format of *Doctor Who* underwent subtle changes with an early priority being the gradual phasing-out of the historicals.

Undoubted, though, Innes Lloyd's greatest gamble was his decision to revamp the series by changing its lead actor and introducing more trendy, up-to-the-minute companions. Daleks aside, by 1966 even the science fiction wonders unveiled in each new futuristic story were breeding feelings of audience discontent brought on by three years of over-familiarity. The very intelligently written Ian Stuart Black serial 'The Savages' brought down very many adverse comments in the wake of a viewing assessment scarcely much different to that of 'The Romans':

| A+ | A | B | C | C− |
|----|-----|-----|-----|-----|
| 5% | 27% | 37% | 18% | 13% |

'At least this particular adventure wasn't one of those boring historical ones and it was miles better than that awful Wild West affair but even so I couldn't work up much interest. The plain truth of the matter is I've got tired of the series which I think is overdue for a long rest.'

This comment was typical of the majority, rather unenthusiastic responses to this, the latest of *Doctor Who*'s adventures in space and time, and to the series as a whole. Even if this was the sort of adventure they preferred, in that the action had taken place in the future rather than the past, and even if, considered dispassionately, the story compared favourably with most of *Doctor Who*'s previous expeditions into the future, many viewers in the sample admitted that they had lost their appetite for a series which, in their opinion, had gone on far too long.

At the same time not a few of these viewers remarked that their children were certainly *not* losing interest: 'The kids liked this adventure and said it was "super-smashing", but then they still think the series is marvellous, unlike me, who tired of it long since.' And there were plenty of adult viewers who evidently still have a taste for this 'imaginative' and 'exciting' serial. According to this group, this particular expedition had been 'one of *Doctor Who*'s most eventful, thrilling and exciting to date.'

The solution was change and, ironically in one respect, a case of the wheel turning full circle. *Doctor Who* had been conceived as a series for older children/young adults. Its early years, however, had seen a much wider expansion of appeal and a proving of Sydney Newman's theories about the attraction of intelligent, plain-statement story-telling. The threat had come only when the series, in turn, had tried to expand to be all things to all audiences – attempting comedy ('The Romans'), Shakespeare ('The Crusade'), and even nursery rhyme ('The Celestial Toymaker').

What Innes Lloyd advocated, and ultimately did, was a return to David Whitaker's more limited spectrum of audience appeal, re-establishing the rich mythology of the series with its simple tales of men versus monsters, one of the oldest forms of story-telling in existence. 'I want *Doctor Who* to have less obvious history, more guts,' was Lloyd's most widely-quoted comment about how he saw the future of the series. He intended the show should return to apealing directly to a young, perceptive teenage audience, with adults and smaller children invited along only if they cared to join in.

For Newman, who was intrumental in the re-thinking and recasting of *Doctor Who*, this was full circle vindication of the views he had expressed, summing up on the *Pathfinders in Space* experiment:

'The writer and the Producer may have to recognise that there are only two groups – the young and the old, the less perceptive and the perceptive. In short, the teenager may be immature, but he must be regarded as being just as intelligent and perceptive as an adult. He demands the same high degree of writing, acting, directing and production polish as his parents.'

The future for the next Doctor was bright indeed.

# APPENDIX

## The Hartnell Years

| CODE | SERIAL TITLE | WRITERS | DIRECTORS | DESIGNERS |
|---|---|---|---|---|
| **Produced by Verity Lambert and Mervyn Pinfield** | | | | |
| **Script editor: David Whitaker** | | | | |
| A | An Unearthly Child (The Tribe of Gum) | Anthony Coburn (C. E. Webber) | Waris Hussein | Peter Brachaki Barry Newbery |
| B | The Daleks | Terry Nation | Christopher Barry Richard Martin | Raymond Cusick Jeremy Davies |
| C | Beyond the Sun (The Edge of Destruction) | David Whitaker | Richard Martin Frank Cox | Raymond Cusick |
| D | Marco Polo | John Lucarotti | Waris Hussein John Crocket | Barry Newbery |
| E | The Keys of Marinus | Terry Nation | John Gorrie | Raymond Cusick |
| F | The Aztecs | John Lucarotti | John Crocket | Barry Newbery |
| G | The Sensorites | Peter R. Newman | Mervyn Pinfield Frank Cox | Raymond Cusick |
| H | The Reign of Terror | Dennis Spooner | Henric Hirsch | Roderick Laing |
| J | Planet of Giants | Louis Marks | Mervyn Pinfield Douglas Camfield | Raymond Cusick |
| K | The Dalek Invasion of Earth | Terry Nation | Richard Martin | Spencer Chapman |
| **Script editor: Dennis Spooner** | | | | |
| L | The Rescue | David Whitaker | Christopher Barry | Raymond Cusick |
| M | The Romans | Dennis Spooner | Christopher Barry | Raymond Cusick |
| **Produced by Verity Lambert** | | | | |
| N | The Web Planet | Bill Strutton | Richard Martin | John Wood |
| P | The Crusade | David Whitaker | Douglas Camfield | Barry Newbery |
| Q | The Space Museum | Glyn Jones | Mervyn Pinfield | Spencer Chapman |
| R | The Chase | Terry Nation | Richard Martin | Raymond Cusick John Wood |
| **Script editor: Donald Tosh** | | | | |
| S | The Time Meddler | Dennis Spooner | Douglas Camfield | Barry Newbery |
| T | Galaxy Four | William Emms | Derek Martinus | Richard Hunt |
| T/A | Mission to the Unknown | Terry Nation | Derek Martinus | Richard Hunt Raymond Cusick |
| **Produced by John Wiles** | | | | |
| U | The Myth Makers | Donald Cotton | Michael Leeston-Smith | John Wood |
| V | The Daleks' Master Plan | Terry Nation Dennis Spooner | Douglas Camfield | Raymond Cusick Barry Newbery |
| W | The Massacre | John Lucarotti Donald Tosh | Paddy Russell | Michael Young |
| **Script editor: Gerry Davis** | | | | |
| X | The Ark | Paul Erickson Lesley Scott | Michael Imison | Barry Newbery |
| **Produced by Innes Lloyd** | | | | |
| Y | The Celestial Toymaker | Brian Hayles | Bill Sellars | John Wood |
| Z | The Gunfighters | Donald Cotton | Rex Tucker | Barry Newbery |
| AA | The Savages | Ian Stuart Black | Christopher Barry | Stuart Walker |
| BB | The War Machines | Ian Stuart Black (Kit Pedler) | Michael Ferguson | Raymond London |
| CC | The Smugglers | Brian Hayles | Julia Smith | Richard Hunt |
| DD | The Tenth Planet | Kit Pedler Gerry Davis | Derek Martinus | Peter Kindred |

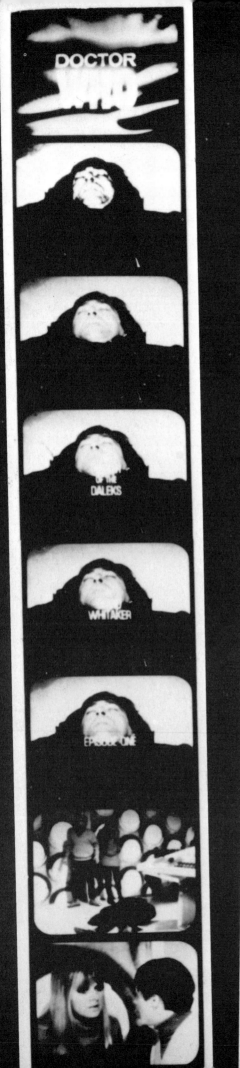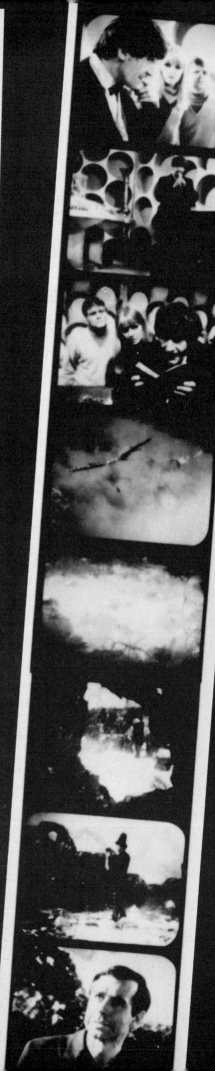

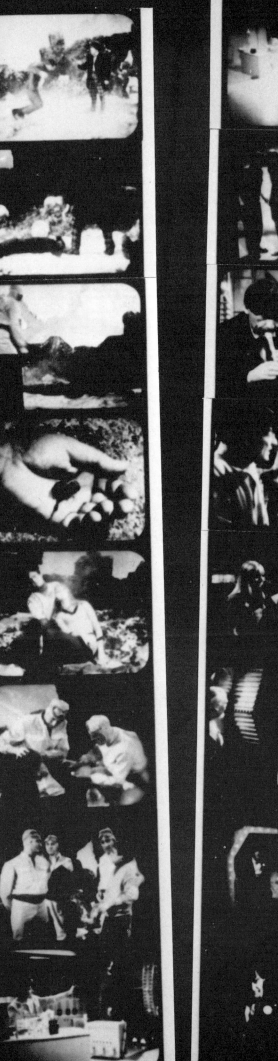

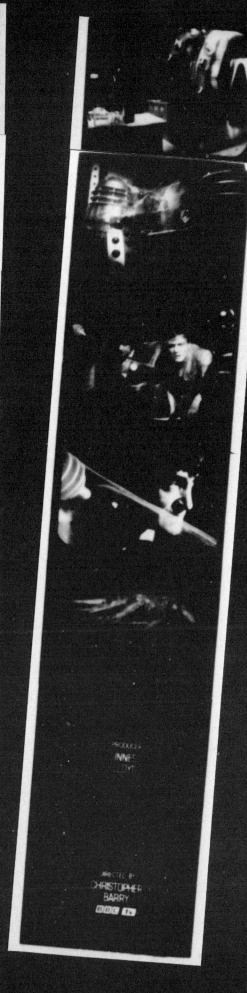

The adventure continues . . .